Love,
Barefoot

The MESSAGE

Vision for a new golden era

BAREFOOT DOCTOR

Imago People TV

First published in 2012.

ISBN 978-0-9571592-0-4

Printed in the United Kingdom for Imago People Publishing by
CPI Group (UK) Ltd, Croydon, CR0 4YY

A CIP Catalogue record for this book is available from the British Library.

Dedicated to the late, great RD Laing – beloved teacher, mentor and friend.

Contents

Introduction

As a leader, a specialist in making people feel good from the inside out, a master of the Taoist martial arts, medicine and meditation systems and the author of 14 previous books, I've been living by and teaching the Taoist system for 40 years and have helped millions transform using these techniques and philosophies. Among the collection of august teachers and gurus I trained with was the eminent maverick psychiatrist RD Laing, to whose memory this book is dedicated and with whom I studied comparative religion (spiritual paths) as well as the machinery of consciousness, with a bias towards the Western perspective. The Bible was at the top of the reading list he gave me.

It has long been my desire to reframe the Ten Commandments as the underpinnings for a new world. And as well as the time now being right for the world to hear THE MESSAGE, in my own development as a teacher and communicator, my handle on the inner methods has now reached a commensurate level to do it justice.

According to our own Western, pagan-infused, Judeo-Christian mythology, Moses, described as liberator and leader of the Israelites but probably an initiate of the Egyptian mysteries, went up on

Mount Sinai, had a conference with God and came down with a set of stone tablets inscribed with ten commandments, adherence to which would enable society to function optimally and thus bring it to the so-called Promised Land.

This is allegory, including even the commandments themselves.

The liberation of a people from slavery alludes to the liberation of the self from delusion-born suffering. The character of Moses alludes to the guiding spirit within or, in modern terminology, the subconscious.

The promised land alludes, if not to a full-blown utopia, which is unrealistic in any case, then at least to an enlightened global society governed more by wisdom and trust than foolishness or suspicion, inclined more towards collaboration and cooperation than domination or oppression, in which love, honor and respect comprise the currency and the economy it drives is booming, enabling an unprecedented flowering of the human spirit benefiting everyone on Earth and ensuring we not only survive this most challenging transitional passage but actually thrive by it.

The Ten Commandments themselves allude to the ten ethical principles of natural grace, arising endogenously, spontaneously and automatically once the individual is internally aligned and centered, and thus in command of themselves. The 'thou shalt not' and 'thou shalt' approach to influencing people doesn't even work with children, let alone adults. Treating the Ten Commandments as actual commandments is evidently nonsensical, as the very establishment which claims to follow them itself ordains and partakes of murder (at times of war), robbery (colonising territories) and lying (disinformation and hypocrisy) on a grand scale.

And Moses represents that aspect of your psyche that yearns to lead you home, to oneness with all that is – the enlightened, transcendent state.

We are obliged now to stop pretending to be irresponsible children with a set of commandments to break and to rise up collectively to the magnificent fullness of who we really all are: ineffable presences in human form – fallen angels nearing the end of a long journey home.

Doing so, learning to follow these ten precepts for enlightenment, we will indeed, circumstances permitting, enter the Promised Land. We will collectively meet the challenge, come through the crisis and move as one to the next evolutionary stage, potentially the most exciting step the human race has ever taken.

This is THE MESSAGE and the time has come to spread it far and wide to every corner of the Earth.

On the ride this book facilitates, we take the Ten Commandments and reposition them in light of the above, from a Taoism-informed, humanism-based perspective and so derive a feasible, effective and necessary template for a new world.

For instance, once we've each woken up to who and what we really are – and, by extension, who and what everyone really is – we will not be so inclined to kill or want to kill, nor even to violate another. This extends to being less inclined to want to kill or violate another's spirit, energy, creativity, enthusiasm, self-respect, self-esteem and so on.

Nor will we be so inclined to steal from another – not just possessions or lovers, but ideas and, more importantly, energy.

Nor, for example, will we be so inclined to place any other gods before the One (the Tao, the primordial presence). We'll not be so held in thrall by the gods of consumerism, prestige, vanity or the arcane dogmatic convolutions of formalised outdated religions from a past age.

Included in this book, and essential to the discussion on the Ten Commandments, are detailed instructions for attaining to and maintaining the requisite internal set-up to engender the transcendent state.

Together these methods comprise the underlying empowerment template of the ancient Taoists, as passed down through their martial arts, medicine and meditation systems, collectively constituting possibly the most evolved, developed, sophisticated, powerful and straightforward of all the ancient disciplines.

Section I

Why Am I Writing This?

This is not a self-help book.

The self has been helped enough already, via a vast body of books appealing to the more self-centric, greedy aspects of human nature: get rich, get a lover, be a better lover, get a partner, get the house you want, get the job you want, make better decisions, be more popular, market yourself better and so on.

This is a humanity-help book.

But though it would be utterly grand if all 7 billion people on Earth bought this book so I could buy a modest planet with a pleasant view in a distant galaxy somewhere and retire to it, it in fact only requires a relatively small minority of the global herd to go with the notion herein, to instigate a meta-shift for everyone.

Scientists were observing the apes that lived on a group of atolls off the coast of Japan and subsisted on a potato-like vegetable. One day one of the apes accidentally dropped his potato in the sea, which washed the soil off it, and ate it. Noting it tasted better this way, he went down to the shore each day to wash his potato. Before long, one by one, all the other monkeys started copying. And at the point at which a hundred monkeys were going down to the beach each day to wash their potatoes, without any obvious form of communication between the atolls, all the monkeys on all the atolls spontaneously began washing their potatoes in the sea.

It's the same with fashion. Back in the early 90s, kids in North London were borrowing their older brothers' jeans to go skateboarding, the bigger size providing more comfort, which often led to their underwear showing over the top of the waistband. This caught on by and by until, without even knowing why, this utterly stupid fashion had spread ubiquitously around the world.

In other words, no matter how sensible or how daft, once the number of followers of any idea reaches the magic critical mass point, it tips the trend from a select few to the masses, without the masses having a clue why.

Section 2

The Ten Commandments, Reframed

The original Ten Commandments were allegedly dropped as two stone tablets into the hands of Moses by God. Hocus-pocus aside, they actually provide the perfect template for enlightenment – the inner angelic state that facilitates the possibility of us all living together in an unprecedented state of mutual tolerance, love and harmony.

Before issuing the commandments, God says: "I am the Lord your God."

If you strip away the lord aspect, which derived from a manipulated translation of the Bible at a time England had only just recently moved on from a feudal society, you get "I am God".

Look around you now: the sky above you, the ground beneath your feet, and all the bits in between. Experience yourself in relation to it all, in relation to the infinite continuum of life manifest here on the Earth-plane, and imagine it as a single entity, or as a manifestation of a single entity. Imagine that entity speaks to you on the subtle level through the sound of the OM (AUM) (see page 115) and says in a voice neither male nor female but both at the same time, "I am God", or, if you prefer, "I am the Tao."

This in itself is the primary key to enlightenment.

Because as soon as you can see all aspects of the manifest world – this world of people and machines, this world of nature, this world of planets, stars and galaxies, this world of infinite space, and this world of you – as an expression of the ineffable background presence, as the Tao throwing shapes on the dance floor of the universe, you are no longer fooled or perturbed by appearances.

So that no matter how thrilling or scary your circumstances in any given moment, no matter how scintillating or distracting the current configuration of details, you remain centered, referenced to and identified with the prime cause informing it all and are thus able to maintain equilibrium and perspective at all times. You are able to receive and process the endless incoming stream of information as an expression of absolute love, life and consciousness, as an expression of God or the Tao talking to you – talking to you in the wind, in the sound of the waves, in the sound of the traffic passing by, in the sound of people talking, in the sound of music, in the hum of the fridge, in the color of someone's shirt, in the moans of ecstasy of someone you're making love to, even in the disturbing sound of someone being angry, or in the deadly silence of bombs dropping from the sky. All of it – the sound of creation, sustenance and destruction – is the background presence talking to you, the OM (AUM).

Knowing yourself primarily in relation to the OM, you naturally desist from grasping at the anxiety or excitement in the play of external events and their impact on your psyche.

No longer grasping at either anxiety or excitement, you are at peace. When you have peace, you are complete in yourself regardless of circumstance.

Paradoxically, complete in yourself you naturally attract the circumstances you need to complete you, because the outside invariably reflects the inside. So not only do you enjoy the ineffable boons of equilibrium and perspective, not only do you enjoy being complete as you are, you also automatically manifest an external set of circumstances to support your completeness by way of reflection.

Remember: external life, the manifest world, is but a mirror that reflects back at you whichever state you project onto it. Project completeness and you receive completeness, or whatever it takes to support the state of completeness, from without.

You know yourself as an expression of the background presence, an expression of God. And you know everyone and everything else as an expression of the background presence, an expression of God, too. You know it all as a resonance of OM.

This is what the Taoists mean when they suggest the way to gain the entire universe is to invest in loss. Lose your attachment to the myth of who you think you are; lose your attachment to the myth of who you think other people are; lose your attachment to the myth of what you think the world is; and you arrive at the background presence informing you, them and it. You arrive at God, your arrive at the Tao. Of course, you'd never left it in the first place – you just imagined you had, hence the need for keys to break the spell and bring you back to where you were anyway.

The Buddha suggested desire was the root of all suffering. At first this may seem anathema to being alive, as desire is surely the very driving force of humanity: you desire to live, so you breathe, you desire to eat, so you find food (or you die), you desire love, so you find people. Without this drive nothing would happen: there'd be no stories, no entertainment; there'd be no disappointment when you didn't get what you desired; there'd be no pain of loss when the object of desire was inevitably removed from you. And it would be dreadfully dull. But it'll never happen anyway. Desire is intrinsic and essential to life.

However, what the Buddha might well have gone on to say, but which he implied in all his teachings in any case, was that once you hear God talking to you through everyone and everything, once you discern the background presence, the Tao, informing all phenomena, once you've trained your senses to perceive the OM behind the myriad of surface facades comprising the world of matter, you naturally tend to direct your desire exclusively to union with it, to communion; you naturally yearn to be at one with it. Or, more precisely, you naturally yearn to divest yourself of all grasping at illusions and so constantly reveal your oneness with it.

This level of desire does not lead to suffering. To the contrary, channeling the thrust driving all your desire into the desire for communion with all that is, and the consequent transcendence that inevitably elicits, vanquishes all suffering in a trice.

Eventually, even this is recognised as a mere tool, a device to turn off the illusion. The more you know yourself as God, the more identified you are with the prime cause of existence as opposed to its external effects, the less you need to desire to be at one with it, until eventually, there is no desire – just oneness.

In itself, if fully understood and appreciated, this would have been enough. "I am God, I am the Tao, I am the background presence informing all of this, I am the OM" would have been sufficient information to enlighten the whole world till the end of time. But presumably God was aware of humanity's propensity for complicating things based on a mistrust of simple axioms, so He went on to enumerate how this enlightened perspective might play out on the ground in real time. For this He used Moses, symbolic of that aspect of your psyche that yearns for communion and so is drawn to provide steps.

The first five commandments concern you rectifying and sustaining your relationship with the background presence – the OM, the God, the Tao. The second five concern you rectifying and sustaining your relationship with humanity.

Jesus, symbolic of the enlightened state, compressed the ten into two on this basis: love (be open to and mindful of) God, the Tao, the OM, the presence, with all your heart, soul and might (with all aspects of you, so that you know yourself as it and it as you); and love others as you love yourself (as God, the Tao, the OM, the presence).

But this evidently didn't strike enough of a chord to cut through humanity's propensity for complicating (and distorting) things either, so then along came Barefoot and reframed the original ten in a last-ditch effort before it's too late (if it isn't already, in which case we can treat the following as merely interesting entertainment while we hang around en masse waiting to die).

Commandment/Principle/ Precept One

Thou shalt have no other gods before me.

Taken literally, you'd be forgiven for forming the impression that the Tao is a petulant child or dictator insisting you see her or him as number one in the charts and don't ever dare see her or him otherwise.

But taking the story literally is nonsensical self-delusion.

However, taken as a precept for enlightenment or principle of grace, this first commandment provides the most important guideline of all.

When centered and hence in the enlightened, undistracted, non-obfuscated state – in communion with the OM, the Tao, the God, the background presence, wherein you know all form to be merely passing expression of the one prime source – you can't fail to place that relationship above all others. You can't fail to cleave to it through thick and thin, and wouldn't consider any other relationship more important, even for a moment. Not for a single instant would you become confused enough to place any of the lesser gods before the Tao.

Safety. Security. Money. Status. Comfort. Temporal power. Houses. Possessions. Good looks. Sex. Romantic love. Success. Popularity. Self-importance. Pleasure. Intellectual prowess. Physical prowess. Shoes. Shopping as an activity in general. Socialising. Ideology. Creative pursuits. Being right. Being clever.

...a few of the lesser gods to whom we've tended to award greater importance and significance than the OM informing them all.

And there's nothing wrong and, indeed, potentially everything right about each and every one of them. But yin and yang still governs them all, so no matter how much of any of them you manage to obtain at any one time, you'll inevitably also equally experience the flip side associated with each. Safety brings stasis and boredom. Security breeds insecurity. Money brings responsibilities. Status isolates and in any case is easily lost. Comfort robs you of adventure. Temporal power opens you to competition. Houses need maintenance. Possessions need looking after. Good looks fade. Sex causes complications. Romance dwindles. And so on.

Nothing external, nothing manifest provides the unequivocal peace and completeness you crave.

The only thing which provides that is identifying with and adhering to the underlying presence informing all external phenomena and so eliciting perpetual communion with the continuum, the OM.

But there's no commandment capable of forcing you into that state. You can try and obey it as a commandment but you'll fail again and again, as witnessed by society's failure in this respect ever since Moses first moseyed down the mountain to take his tablets to the people – sure, keep taking those tablets, Moses, but it really won't do the required job.

However, if you attain and maintain the enlightened state by centering yourself again and again and training your eye to spy the presence behind the form at all times, by and by you'll find you naturally *want* to keep the Tao (the OM, the God etc, etc) as number one before all lesser gods. It becomes more and more daft not to.

You'll naturally find yourself opening to (loving) the presence with all your heart, all your soul and all your might. Not because Moses, Jesus, God or anyone else told you to, but because it ultimately becomes the only way to order, make sense of and thrive on your existence.

You learn, in the fullness of time, to relax your belly (seat of your might), your chest (heart) and midbrain region (soul or consciousness access point) and so let the essence of love flow from you to the all and from the all back into you, and to let this up-and-down-the-connection flow be central to every moment as you wend your way along the Great Thoroughfare of life.

Not because you're *meant to,* but because it's the only viable way to get reality to sit right within and around you.

And indeed it does when you do.

When you can look around you at the entire confluence of all the people, situations, events, phenomena, feelings and thoughts comprising what you perceive as the world, and (choose) to see it all – both the external and internal – as the Tao talking to you, loving you with all its heart, soul and might, and when you are are willing to love it likewise in return, all your existential and temporal fear and dread dissolve and the deepest clarity dawns. The effect is a total reset, whereby everything starts anew, causing conditions to spontaneously assume an elegance of shape and motion that could never be contrived by human hand.

Again, this is the basis of the Taoist *wu wei* system of manifesting: manifest the Tao, the presence and all the rest will be added to you. *Seek ye peace and all the rest will be added*.

This, of course, implies taking responsibility. No longer can you delude yourself that you're a victim of circumstance. You are instead obliged to accept that it's you who commands the tone and look of how life shapes up for you.

Which is precisely why the original set of ten came through as commandments: it must have been assumed people weren't capable of taking responsibility. So instead commandments were issued, which would inevitably be broken again and again, often in the most hypocritical way by the very people whose authority was vested in the imaginary god who carved the imaginary letters into the imaginary tablets of stone. (The stone and carving thereon, incidentally, alludes to the primordial, eternal, universal and ultimately irrevocable nature of these ten precepts.)

However, as per the underlying theme – the message of *The Message* – we have now presumably reached a high enough level of collective evolution to assume responsibility and therefore have no further need of playing the childish game of issuing and breaking rules. At least this book's purpose is to propose that we have, wildly optimistic though this may be.

In practice, centering-born enlightenment is an ongoing process – like me – you may find yourself flipping in and out of it, variously distracted by the lesser gods of temporal existence. This oscillation between the enlightened and deluded state gradually accelerates until, like the frames of a film giving the appearance of a continuous stream of images, you experience enlightenment (the hugely more powerful of the two poles) as a constant stream or as the default position. It's then safe to say you'll not be mistakenly putting any other gods before God, the Tao, the Great Blah.

(I use Blah not pejoratively but merely to allude to the nonsense of making names sacrosanct – but more of that soon when we come to the third commandment.)

Commandment/Precept/ Principle Two

Thou shalt not make any graven image or idol of the Lord your God, not of anything in the heavens above, in the earth beneath nor in the waters beneath the earth.

I occasionally used to go into the church in the village I lived in, in Catalunya (a region in North East Spain), the saint of which was Santa Reparada, meaning *she who repairs everything even before it's broken*. I'd sit there and gaze at her statue, her graven image, stare into her eyes and by concentrating could make the world around vanish into a haze, while downloading the essence of preemptive repair her name promised into my circuitry.

I was aware I was employing a cheap fairground trick to elicit the required state of healing but there's nothing intrinsically wrong with a trick or two every now and then. However had I grown dependent on this device, it would have eventually left me wanting. Had I not had as my existential bedrock this Taoist-humanistic template, I'd have eventually become dependent on a statue instead of plugging directly into a source.

And that's the point. This commandment has been blatantly broken again and again by the very people who purport to base their ethos on the Ten Commandments – think of how many Jesus, Mary or saint statues there must be in the world, for instance.

And the Buddhists are no better.

Mistaking dolls for the divine, and investing energy in them as such, is deluded. It's not wrong. It's merely primitive and misguided. It's a sin – not in the sense of a misdemeanor requiring punishment, but in the literal sense of missing the mark and hitting the edge of the target rather than the bull's eye at the center. It's an off-centered way of being.

The very first line of the *Tao Te Ching* – book of the Way and its virtue, granddaddy of all Taoist literature – states that the Tao that is the true Tao cannot be named, cannot be described and cannot be defined; it can merely be pointed to.

As you grow in your center-born enlightenment you realise more and more that you cannot explain, describe, define or depict the prime cause, the Tao, the God, the Great Blah, simply because it's too big, too ubiquitous, too all-informing and too unfathomable, and that even to try is a waste of time.

Furthermore, to invest in a statue, even if it purportedly sheds real tears, is depriving your existential underpinnings of true substance or validity.

You naturally learn to see the Tao in everyone and everything around you and have no need to focus all your attention on a human-made object of any kind, as this will merely limit the scope of your communion with it.

This extends even to another person. If you grant someone the power to sustain your joy and wellbeing and delude yourself into believing them to be anything more than a passing form expressing the presence for a relatively brief while, you will inevitably be bereft when they let you down, leave you or die on you. Honor and love them with all your heart, of course, but as an expression of the presence rather than as the presence itself. In other words, be wary of making your loved ones into living graven images of the divine. By the same token, be wary of letting vanity encourage you to make a graven image of your own form, as do those who carve, inject, sculpt and paint their features into a different shape.

All forms pass over time. No form – no matter how gorgeous – is the source itself; it is merely an expression of the source. The more you attach yourself to form, the more you invite the pain of loss when that form inevitably changes or passes.

However, the more you identify with the underlying presence informing all forms including yours, the more resilience and equanimity you'll be imbued with as you wend your way through the often ferocious reality of human life, with all its comings and goings.

This second commandment, then, is a development of the first: the more centered, awake and enlightened you are, the more you naturally desist from investing in any particular form – including your own body – that might detract from knowing yourself as one with the continuum, and the less you presume to be able to define, depict, describe or explain the presence, simply because that would be to limit it and drag it down to human scale.

In Genesis, it states that God made man in His own image. I suggest they got that the wrong way round, either in translation or in the original text. Surely it's man who made God in *his* own image.

The message of The Message posits that we've just about now reached the stage of evolution whereby we no longer need to commit that stupidity; we no longer need to anthropomorphise the presence; no longer need to put a face on the causative factor behind anything in the heavens above, in the earth beneath or in the waters beneath the earth; that doing so runs directly counter to enlightenment.

God has no face. That's why it creates you and me – to give itself a face it can wear to market.

These faces we have, along with all the implausible shapes the Tao is throwing on the dance floor of existence, are enough to remind us of the presence without needing to resort to dolls or any other visual device.

Commandment/Principle/ Precept Three

Thou shalt not take the name of the Lord thy God in vain.

Well, just like the others this one got broken from the start: all the wars of religion, of mass killing in the name of God; all the mealy-mouthed hypocrisy and barefaced lies in the name of God; all the daylight robbery in the name of God; and all the mass con-tricks pulled on all the poor, innocent, indigenous people around the world, conscripted and hypnotised by clever colonialist conjurors into funding organised religion; even the instigation and marketing of the three main religions in the name of God in the first place was breaking this one.

The name of God, in fact, has probably been taken in vain more than any other name there is.

In God we trust.

What, to create an entire society based on mass psychosis?

Even Moses himself, carrying the tablets of stone down Mount Sinai to the naughty children of Israel dancing round the golden calf (the god of materialism), and saying the tablets were inscribed by God, was breaking this commandment.

However, when you look at number three from the enlightened perspective, a different picture emerges.

When you know yourself as an expression of the presence and therefore know everyone else as an expression of it too, you naturally intuit an inherent flow to events resulting from the interaction between you and others, which seems to have a will of its own – call it the will of God, or the will of the greater good if you like.

So rather than attempt to force your will, your ideas of what *should* be, on others, you merely set an intention for the highest possible good to emerge from every situation and confluence of situations for everyone (including you, of course). Then you relax, regroup and allow the Tao to do whatever it does, trusting that through all the twists and turns, ups and downs, fortunes and misfortunes, triumphs and failures, the highest good will indeed ensue in its own sweet, unpredictable way.

No longer needing to foist your way on others, no longer needing to persuade or coerce others to bend to your will, you no longer need use dark magic in any form whatsoever, including the darkest form of magic of all: suggesting your will is divinely inspired or ordained and exhorting others to follow it in any of the various names we ascribe to the presence (even if what you're willing is benign).

It's not that doing something in any of the names of the presence is intrinsically wrong; it's just that it's childish and stupid.

And the more enlightened you get, the less you'll be inclined to do it.

In fact the less you'll be inclined to subscribe to any such superstitious practice whatsoever.

Doing things in the name of God belongs to the realm of primitive magic.

As we evolve to the next stage, this will no longer be necessary.

In the new world we're manifesting through, and as a response to our collective evolution, the regressive trends towards organised religion and dogma of all kinds stand a good chance of being relegated to the annals of antiquity altogether, but only if enough of us reach and maintain the state of enlightenment.

I'd even venture to say that the absurd spread of interest in the cheap fairground trick of channeling specific spirits, albeit well-intentioned, might also fall away with all the rest of the cynical ploys foisted on the weak, gullible and unsuspecting.

With enough evolution, we'll stop needing to use all such hocus-pocus and simply say what needs to be said without reference to divine or other-worldly ordination. After all, this entire moving picture show is divinely ordained, so how can we segregate certain bits of it and call them special? It's a risible example of absolute nonsense.

Imagine a world where no hocus-pocus is used in an attempt to influence people; where no one bothers or is drawn to use any of the names of the Tao to justify their beliefs or actions.

I know it's hard, but imagine it anyway – it can happen.

In fact, imagine a world where beliefs themselves are recognised as mere opinions, none of them sacrosanct in themselves – where it's recognised that the boons of enlightenment derive solely from being centered and awake and have nothing whatsoever to do with beliefs of any kind.

Commandment/Precept/ Principle Four

Remember the Sabbath day and keep it holy.

The Sabbath day Jesus would have remembered and kept holy was Saturday, as Jesus was not a Christian but a Jew. It was Saul (who became Paul) who took the ideas and stories of Jesus, ran with them and turned the entire package into one of the most, if not the most, successful, long-lasting brands in history.

Obviously his enterprise received an enormous boost when, much later, Emperor Constantine of Rome adopted Christianity as the official religion there. It was he who decreed that the Sabbath would thenceforth fall on Sunday instead.

The Sabbath traditionally required doing no work whatsoever, engaging in no commerce of any kind (including visits to out-of-town shopping malls or DIY stores) and not even attending to basic survival-related tasks such as cooking or washing. It was intended as a total cut-off day in which all your attention was withdrawn from the foreground and focused instead on the background presence. You were encouraged to pray (commune) and hang out with your loved ones from sundown on Friday to sundown on Saturday.

But again, this was allegorical and meant as a reminder to keep every day holy, to see every day as a holiday (originally *holy day*). Rather than get lost in the trance of the workaday world, it would help you to retain awareness at all times of the presence within and around you and everyone, even though you were immersed in daily tasks and obligations.

But as it was probably reckoned at the time, the general populace isn't necessarily so adept at multitasking at this profound level, even though it's incredibly simple to do once you know how. A special day was therefore needed to train us in letting go.

This evidently proved to be too much of a drag for most, hence why we've finally reverted to form and made Sunday one of the busiest days of the week, at least for shopping and traffic.

So as a commandment, this one's as broken as all the rest.

But as an allegory, it perhaps stands in its implications as one of the most salient of all. In light of the ever-burgeoning task-load and accompanying stress of our current global set-up, we need to learn to hold fast to the center while all about us swirls faster and faster.

We need, more than ever, to learn to treat each day as a holy day, a holiday – perhaps an intense, activity-based holiday but a holiday nonetheless.

Not because I'm advocating Peter Pan- or Wendy-ism, but because we deal far more effectively with everything internally and externally when we're enjoying it.

Treating each day as a holiday or holy day, even one spent engaged in the business of everyday life, reminds you that this is your time, your day, no one and nothing else's. This discreet act of repositioning is enough to keep you energised and empowered.

However, there's more to it than just being energised and empowered. Remember that behind the façade of the everyday world, behind the trance of days of the week, before the overlay of human concepts on the ineffable, there are no days of the week. There aren't even any weeks. The whole notion is merely an illusion from start to finish. Another nonsense we've subscribed to without thinking. Another trance we've fallen into unwittingly.

When you really examine it carefully, perhaps with the help of a friendly quantum physicist, you see that the whole notion of linear time itself is merely a fantasy, a construct devised and contrived by us.

However if someone suggested such a thing to the majority of people, I'm sure they'd be called insane, so fixed and convincing is the trance.

Having seen through the illusion, if only for a glimpse, you notice that where we are, or rather when we are, is in an eternal moment – it goes on forever and ever.

Time, as we've grown accustomed to knowing it, is merely a trick-of-the-light style medium the Tao facilitates to prevent everything happening at once and so avoiding a huge, unintelligible collision and mess, just as is the medium of space.

But from where it sits, there is no time. And from where it sits within you, there is no time. Just as from where it sits within everyone there is no time.

This implies that every day for everyone is holy – beneath the surface doings in the mundane realm, behind the disguise of the butcher, the baker and the candlestick maker, is the Tao sitting for eternity in the present moment.

And if that all sounds like so much gobbledygook, it doesn't matter. One day, with enough meditation (centering) practice, maybe it won't.

What matters is the sense of honoring the sacredness of everyone's time, of honoring the presence within them for whom there is no time.

Just contemplating this for a second induces a subtly altered perspective and affords you a sneak view of the Tao behind its outer mantle – the one presence informing and connecting us all.

That's the point of the Sabbath, which according to Jewish mysticism is considered to be the 'bride of God' – the goddess, in other words.

It signifies time devoted to feeling the nurturing background presence.

And as we evolve, as we become more centered, more authentic in our function as conduits of the presence, we'll naturally spontaneously keep not just one day but every day holy. Or, more precisely, we'll stop forgetting that all days are already holy.

Implicit in this always-on awareness that each and every moment is holy is the presence, the Tao, the God, the OM. It is something to be celebrated rather than resisted in fear or ignored in a trancelike state.

And knowing this is so for everyone elicits a natural respect for other people's time, especially when they're devoting it to you.

It's merely a matter of a slight shift of perception.

The trance of the everyday world – that deluded mind-state that causes you to overlook the essential miracle of being alive – works, psycho-spatially speaking, by pulling your attention into the front of your body and skull; into your face, throat, chest and belly.

The enlightened state causes you to sink back inside enough to feel both the back and the front of you. So that rather than being with only half of you, you're with all of you; rather than being enthralled exclusively by the external world, you're held in thrall by the presence within as well.

As we evolve now, we'll find ourselves naturally occupying the rear of our persons as much as the frontal aspect and it's this that will both instigate and reflect the opening of the rear part of the brain.

As this develops there'll be less and less need to denote any particular day as especially holy or sacred – not even Christmas. All days will be holy, all moments holy.

Commandment/Precept/ Principle Five

Thou shalt honor thy mother and father.

This, on the surface, would seem a much easier commandment to keep – you'd imagine most people would naturally honor their mammy and their pappy, or at least call them once a week.

However it's easy to overlook the miracle of life your parents facilitated for you and to disregard the amazing sacrifices they made on your behalf, even if they did an apparently shitty job of it.

The fact is, if you're here reading this your parents did their job well enough. The fuck-ups you're inevitably riddled with, as are we all, most of which you inherited from the inevitable distortions in your parents' make-up, are no reason not to honor the gift of life they afforded you.

Life is necessarily flawed. With every glimmer of light comes a blot of shadow; with every silver lining comes a cloud; with every boon comes a responsibility; with every yang comes a yin.

There is no idyll, save in the imagination.

And it's these very flaws that give life its bite, without which it would all just be one long, tedious, meaningless journey through a sort of nondescript existential sludge, devoid of dynamics, devoid of challenge, devoid of growth potential, devoid, therefore, of fascination.

It's these very flaws in your own psyche that make you the fascinating person you are, and it's your constant challenge in overcoming or healing these flaws that lends your journey direction.

As well you know.

But there's more to it than that.

Once you transcend the commandment level and emerge into the enlightened state through consistent practice of centering over time, you can't fail to honor your mother and father, not just because they gave you life and one way or another facilitated your being here right now, but because you're so naturally appreciative of the miracle of being alive that you honor the vessels that brought you into the world.

And not just your mother and father but all your ancestors stretching back over the past 200,000 years or so, the combined efforts of whom contributed to every facet of your person, as well as providing a precedent upon which our entire global infrastructure and support system has been developed (albeit a structure and system facing its possible dissolution at this time).

And not just your ancestors, but the ancestors of everyone alive.

There's a reason many of the world's indigenous peoples engage in ancestor worship. By attuning and giving thanks to the ancestors for facilitating the onward thrust of life enough for you to be here and for paving the way from the primordial state to the structures, systems, luxuries and comforts we enjoy today, it helps set things in perspective and encourages transcendence from the humdrum with all its rises and falls. There's no question that by honoring your ancestors you derive a particular kind of power, a thrust from behind that helps fuel you through your mundane challenges.

And by honoring the ancestors of everyone, you get a glimpse of how connected we all are; how, at root, we derive from and give human expression to the one life-force, the Tao, the God, the OM, the presence.

Which is significant, because each time you catch a glimpse of this universal unity winking back at you, you trigger a subtle yet actual shift in the very warp and weft of the underlying subatomic field, which in consequence benignly affects the surface level.

Forgive me not going into specifically why or how – you can derive that information more efficiently from any friendly quantum physicist. I'm an existential pragmatist, so suggest you instead do the centering technique all day, every day and over time. As the incidence of glimpses increases naturally as a result, you'll see why and how for yourself. But why and how don't matter anyway. Because the experience of catching a glimpse of the Tao winking at you is in itself so instantly rewarding, fulfilling and empowering that you stop caring about *whys* and *hows* and simply revel in the palpable miracle of being alive amidst such an unfathomable mystery.

By the same token, the more enlightened you grow, the more you naturally honor the children too – not just your own but all children. You start to see yourself as mother or father to all children (and that means children of all ages, from 0 to 100 – we're all children behind our adult masks, after all).

Honouring your children means respecting the fact that they're closer to source than you are, having more recently left the undifferentiated state, the pure Tao, and respecting the fact that each is an expression of the Tao in his or her own right, rather than a mere extension of your own ego and life-plan. It means honouring the fact that they each have their own path to follow and that your role is merely to protect and guide to the best of your ability, rather than to control and influence with all your own, often dubious, notions of how things are or should be. It means being authentically *you* with them, rather than merely aping your own parents in a grown-up game of mummies and daddies.

This is obviously not the place to go into a polemic on enlightened parenting, even though I'm sorely tempted to – and I say so humbly as a fairly enlightened father of three amazingly wonderful sons, now men making their own successful contributions to the global mix. I just want to point out that in the enlightened state you naturally tend to honor the sanctity of your children and all the children, and all the children to come, as well as all the ancestors, as symptomatic of your celebration of and respect for the continuum of life.

Yet on a deeper level still, honoring your mother and father implies honoring the primordial yin and yang of existence – the goddess and god, the Great Mother and Great Father of the universe and, as embodied in our neck of the cosmic woods, Mother Earth and Father Sky – honoring the ineffable presence, in other words. Not because you've been commanded to, but because once enlightened, once centered, you can't fail to.

This is all pointing to developing greater and greater awareness of us all as a collective, as a vast living organism, as one huge consciousness, the exegesis of which comprises the next stage of human evolution.

Commandment/Precept/ Principle Six

Thou shalt not kill.

Of all the ten, this commandment has been the most flagrantly disobeyed by the very temporal powers whose authority was presumably predicated on the Ten Commandments in the first place and ironically, cynically, in the name of God, through an almost never-ending succession of religiously inspired wars, as well as wars more overtly over wealth, power, resources and land.

If the power of the land tells you that you cannot kill unless it tells you to kill (in the case of war), or if it says that you cannot kill, but then kills you by execution if you do, it's obvious that making such a commandment in the first place is a nonsensical thing to do.

The only true way to teach with any lasting effect is by example. If you show people by example that to kill is permissible – even laudable, in war or in state executions – people will also kill outside those two contexts. Murder under any pretext breeds more murder.

My own relationship with the concept of killing began cognitively at my very first lesson of Aikido at the tender age of 11 with the venerable late Tio Honsai. He immediately explained that to be granted the power to kill an opponent, you must also train in how to heal an opponent. He taught energy healing at the end of each session, which was what got me started on this healing path in earnest in the first place.

The very idea that I was being taught the skills with which I could kill someone with ease, and the responsibility that entailed, sent a cold shiver up my spine and gave me the impetus to learn how to heal people, in order to balance the potentials.

The more I've progressed along the martial arts path – I've been diligently at it for over 45 years now – the more my primal reptilian brain's hold over my reactions has been sublimated and the more I've eschewed violent responses to situations. Fortunately now, I've enough training and experience to diffuse most untoward situations with just a smile or a well-chosen kindly but firm word. At worst I may have to employ a benign neutralising technique – a finger or wrist-lock that causes no pain but affords me a quiet moment in which to explain effectively to the (usually drunken) aggressor that it would be unwise for us to fight. But the violent impulse is still there. It's latent and sublimated, yet it's still there. However, because through training and practice I'm able more or less instantly to recognise the presence within the aggressor, or within someone I perceive as having wronged me, I'm able more or less instantly to take full command of the impulse and diffuse the negative tension between us without recourse to any sort of violence (including the verbal or emotional variety).

Which isn't to say I'm not capable of feeling or showing anger. Indeed, as anyone I'm close to or work with will tell you, I'm not backwards in coming forwards when pissed off. Even being honked at unfairly from the rear by a cab driver in the city only the other day, as I slowed down to let another cab driver rudely push his way in front of me, I was instantly incensed and almost out of my car and ready to confront him in a trice. But my training self-activated in a trice, too. I was able to see him as the Buddha instead of an opponent, and immediately had compassion for his role in the theatre of life as a frustrated cabbie struggling through the traffic, trying to earn a bob or two.

If I can evolve beyond the reactionary impulses of the reptilian brain, we all can.

If I can naturally develop an innate respect for all life, because (if reason were needed) all life is an expression of the same Tao, presence, God, or Great Blah, then everyone can.

But this won't happen by force – force merely breeds more force. It won't occur by commandment – it hasn't yet and it won't in future.

It will only happen through evolution.

And it will take time.

- The desire for revenge is powerful.
- The desire to dominate is powerful.
- The desire to destroy is powerful.

But the power of love – the essence of what develops through training in centering – is even more powerful.

Because it's not nearly as sensationalist as violence and hence doesn't stand out as much, and because it's far more subtle, it'll take its time to emerge as the major driving force amongst us.

Nonetheless, as I say, if it's possible for me – and the examples show that this isn't so in denial of my baser instincts but in accommodation of them – it's possible for everyone.

Eventually this trend will filter all the way to world-leader level, though it could take a couple of hundred years as we rock and roll our way through the current set of challenges. In the meantime, it's down to each of us as individuals, learning to center more and more and in the transcendent state that elicits intent to meet all comers with a peaceful, loving heart and to eschew violence of any kind, and furthermore to intend everyone on Earth to intend so too.

And as we evolve, this growing unwillingness to kill or do harm will also extend to not wanting to kill another's ideas, enthusiasm, creativity or originality.

It may even extend to not wanting to kill mosquitoes that are biting you in the night (though I'll believe that one when I see it).

Ultimately this principle of grace implies enough of us developing such a powerful, unassailable force field of love and respect for all life that it completely overrides the demands of the reptilian brain.

This will be essential, as it's clear many among us are still driven by a predominance of reptilian brain activity, so it'll take time for the evolutionary thrust to pierce through ubiquitously.

However, I believe it's entirely possible that we can eventually reach a stage when we collectively eschew violence of all kinds in favor of a powerfully developed, loving communication that can accommodate expressions of anger without leading to harming each other in any way.

I believe it's possible – not to mention essential – that we'll eventually realise we're all expressions of the same ineffable presence; and in that realization (not just intellectual but visceral) we will instinctively override the violent impulse and allow the love to spread freely amongst us.

As I said, there will always be a shadow side – yin and yang never stop cycling around each other, no matter how evolved we become – but the aspiration must be to individually and collectively outweigh the reptilian response with the enlightened response.

We're actually doing well already in terms of percentages – the amount of people living in a non-warlike state, not committing crimes of violence, not executing people, not assassinating people and not crashing into each other in cars is far, far greater than the amount of people who are thus engaged – but obviously there's far further we can go in this direction.

I've worked fairly extensively with both convicted murderers in various prisons and ex-military personnel who have killed people in battle. The striking commonality, at least among the ones who are not psychotic or in denial, is an overwhelming guilt they can never come to terms with. And I'm talking about both hardened criminals and well-trained, seasoned soldiers.

The enormity of taking a life, of having a victim's blood on your hands, whether directly in the case of convicted criminals or military personnel in warfare, or indirectly in the case of world leaders who give the order to go to war, is not to be underestimated.

The law of cause and effect has it that what you put out you get back, in one form or another. Kill someone and it kills something profound in you.

This even applies if you kill in self-defense. For though it would seem that there would be certain circumstances in which killing your assailant would be the only resort, my training as a martial artist shows me that there are always lesser ways to fully and effectively disarm or neutralise an opponent.

Let us aspire to and evolve towards love and the collective eschewal of violence of any kind.

Commandment/Precept/ Principle Seven

Thou shalt not commit adultery.

(Yeah, right.) This is probably the most broken commandment of all in terms of numbers. I ran a hugely busy healing practice for nearly 20 years and treated approximately 100,000 people in that time, many of whom were married or had been married, and I never failed to be astonished at the high incidence of betrayal and infidelity reported. It seemed that even the most respectable of them, the most morally sound, the most upright, had committed some sort of misdemeanor in this respect.

However, I don't think it's always been this way. Things seemed to change at the end of the 70s – the time someone seemed to pull the romance plug out of the world in all respects, the time innocence was finally lost forever. As the 80s wore on, something cynical infused the air and it grew stronger and stronger and never went away, despite the semi-respite afforded us by the second summer of love in '88 and the false heyday of the 90s. I do still know two couples who have something really healthy-seeming going on, around whom I don't feel the thickness of pretense or the subtle mechanisms of power struggle and control in the air, through whose evident compatibility and mutual respect my faith in monogamous love is restored. I've no doubt there are way more than just two couples like this on the planet, but I suspect that such a phenomenon these days is as rare as winning the lottery. The factors involved in such complete compatibility on all levels are so numerous and varied, it would be unrealistic to expect them to occur as a given.

I also see more and more evidence of highly evolved, existentially refined people coming together in partnership and finding totally new ways of relating, free of possessiveness, manipulation, power struggle and control issues, free of lies and hypocrisy and so able to establish a mutually supportive, nurturing dynamic, at least for as long as it lasts.

For many or most these days, marriage is as outworn an idea as organised religion. It comprises an aspect of the big con – the myth that someone, somewhere, long dead by now, knows better than you about how to live your life at the most fundamental level; and that someone has the authority of God and the tabloid press on his or her side to back it up; and that someone says it's right and proper to formalise your love affair with someone and guarantee exclusivity over your body, heart and soul by ratifying it in law, often supposedly in the eyes of God. Based on the fantastical notion of living happily ever after, despite the mounting, highly unromantic pressures of mundane existence, it's no surprise that the majority of marriages, in the Western world at least, now end in divorce within five years.

Marriage evolved in tribal days as yet another crowd control device, predicated on the man having total control and his wife being more of an economically useful cohort than a partner. As a result, the ostensibly cohesive family unit was easier to control by the tribe, state or relevant authorities than an individual. Millennia later, as women's liberation gave rise to greater and greater gender equality and people were starting to live much longer, this set-up was obviously not going to have the resilience to weather the transition. Even so, though marriage is now on the decline as a trend, people still jump into it blindly or semi-blindly in their droves. Women, being vessels of yin, and yin representing the contractive, structure-seeking tendency, incline more naturally to ratified, formalised structures; while men being vessels of yang, and yang representing the expansive, mobile force, tend more towards being free to roam at will. But as the genders equalise themselves, this yin-yang divide is becoming less obvious – women are becoming more yang as they take their place in the marketplace of daily life and men are becoming more yin as they take on more feminine, nurturing qualities and roles, which, as far as I can see, results in women becoming less circumspect and more open about their adulterous tendencies, and men the reverse.

In any case, women are, and have always been, far better actors than men in this respect, so who knows what's really going on?

Most relatively realistic, sensible men and women I talk to these days, who've understood and accepted the duplicitous aspect of human nature, assume their partner *is* betraying them, and think that's OK as long as they don't find out, it doesn't cost them money, time or heartache, and doesn't disrupt their lives.

This isn't to say it's ideal but that with experience and maturity, it's accepted as more or less inevitable and essentially inconsequential.

And it isn't to say jealously isn't aroused, but that with experience and maturity, jealousy can be experienced, owned and processed without recourse to acting out destructively.

And as I said, there are those couples for whom the compatibility factor is high enough, through whichever combination of karma, fate or pure fluke, to facilitate a genuinely fulfilling, satisfying and even blissful union for both for the duration, and for whom betrayal and infidelity wouldn't even enter the equation. But this appears to be rare these days.

In this (shady old) light it's obvious how commanding people to desist from committing adultery is like pissing in the wind. Naturally, it would be highly undesirable for those tribal leaders of old to have everyone in the tribe openly having sex with everyone else's spouse, as society would have swiftly broken down, so lots of covering up was required; but in our post-modern world, where, on account of technological advances, men and women no longer need each other to tend to their respective survival needs in the same way, the fabric of society is far more able to withstand infidelity without collapsing. Yet the cover-ups and lies are just as rife as ever.

But it's not just marriage. Committed relationships between two partners (man-woman, woman-woman, man-man) are subject to more or less the same set of potential stresses and strains. And while, technically, adultery doesn't apply unless officially married, the urge and the consequence are just as potentially significant.

In essence it boils down to being able to accommodate betrayal somehow.

Betrayal arises from duplicity, which arises from unresolved ambivalence and is apparently intrinsic to the human condition.

However, by learning to center progressively over time, knowing yourself and anyone you choose to consort with is an expression of the Tao, the one presence, it becomes patently clear that betraying another is essentially betraying yourself, by diminishing your sense of who you are at some level and weighing yourself down with both guilt and the anxiety that you may be rumbled.

Not that this stops you, but it allows you to frame and therefore accept the syndrome in a more realistic setting, thus enabling you to observe yourself engaging in betrayal without going into denial. Observing is the first and often the only step required for healing any syndrome.

And by and by, you find yourself only able to enter into any sort of tryst if it allows you the space to be yourself, to be open about what yourself comprises, and even to be honest about the fact you're bound to obfuscate or tell lies at some point; because if you're honest about it, obfuscating and lying are inevitable at some level in all situations for pretty much everyone. For instance: you spot, smile at, flirt with or connect with someone you find compellingly attractive; you get home, your partner hugs you warmly, kisses you and tells you how much she/he loves you. You feel the love, you love the love, you love them back and say "I love you too", and it feels right despite having just had your head turned. You *may* disclose how your head has just been turned, but the chances are that the dynamic feels so comfortingly tender and sweet, you won't want to risk upsetting it with such a disclosure. And you can assume the same for your partner.

And none of it's as important, terrible, wonderful or significant as we all assume. In fact it's all rather ordinary. Ultimately, all that matters is the love you *do* share between you, not the love you don't.

And all that really matters is your relationship with yourself. For the more open and honest, accepting and forgiving you are of yourself – the more you allow yourself to be yourself with yourself – the more your external relationship or relationships will automatically reflect that, or at least the more likely you are to manifest relationships that facilitate your remaining so, rather than hinder it.

So it's not something to be intervened with from the outside in. Eventually it's about you balancing your relationship with yourself and thereby manifesting, by way of reflection, external relationships that are balanced enough to enjoy for at least a while.

And, as I imply, the success of a relationship is not necessarily judged by its duration. Success is also measured by how effectively, either through struggle or through nurturing, you cause each other to transform and grow. Sometimes there's potential for a whole adult lifetime of mutual transformation and growth facilitation. Sometimes there's only potential enough for a short spell.

And what determines this is an utter mystery, whether it's fate, the stars, free will, or the autonomic, biogenetically triggered pheromone exchange between you both, which dictates when you enter each other's orbits and when you exit.

But what we can know is that, as we evolve, our tendency to betray those we consort with intimately decreases – not through willpower or self-discipline; not through performing mental and emotional acrobatics and contortions to quell your desire for someone else so you can focus on your partner and enjoy a pleasant evening watching television together; but because, as you become more at one with yourself and, by extension, with all there is, you naturally manifest more wholesome situations and won't find yourself engaging in anything less in the first place.

But this healing will come about when we finally grow up and accept that betrayal is an ordinary part of the theatre of life and in itself is really not such a big deal. Betrayal generally won't kill you – at least, not quickly enough to worry about.

Come back in another couple of hundred years, however, when we've had time to evolve a bit more and I'll no doubt have a fresh and more incisive slant on this seemingly eternal conundrum.

Commandment/Precept/ Principle Eight

Thou shalt not steal.

The British, presumably feeling they were acting under the auspices of God at the time, stole most of the known world by force. The Spanish stole most of the rest, the British stole directly from the Spanish as they steered their bullion ships home and the bits left over were stolen mostly by Portugal and Holland. All these entities were flying the God flag at the time – the same God who carved the commandments on the stones, including this one about not stealing, and handed them to Moses to give the people.

This was the example set by the establishment.

Yet someone stealing a loaf of bread in those days could be hanged for it.

I was talking to a young woman, a personal assistant to a big player in the global finance industry, earning a relatively big salary – an exemplary PA in most ways, except she felt it was fair game to 'borrow' stationery, petty cash, cab rides, phone lines and other relatively inconsequential bits and pieces, because "the company could afford it." I pointed out that the company, though apparently an entity in its own right, was in fact an extension of her boss, who was not simply a bottomless pit of money; and that as the cost of stationery and sundries increased even just a little bit, he'd eventually have to compensate for it somehow. I asked whether she would like it if bits of her make-up or clothing went missing every now and then because someone fancied 'borrowing' them. She said she wouldn't. I asked her why she imagined it was OK to 'borrow' bits and pieces from him. "Because it's not from him; it's from the company." I asked whence she imagined the 'company' derived its revenue – the revenue to pay her wages for instance. From him, she agreed.

Our complex system of trade, something that's grown organically ever since agriculture enabled our society to grow large enough to need something more sophisticated than straightforward bartering, is delicately balanced. Though stealing stationery might seem a relatively miniscule infringement of the rules, when multiplied by all the people making such miniscule infringements, the effect can eventually be to upend the whole thing, pretty much as we're witnessing now on a global scale.

If, during one morning's rush hour, only the tiniest percentage of people ignored the stop-on-the-red-light rule, an entire city could be brought to gridlock.

You never know when your tiny infringement will be the straw that breaks the camel's back.

Three years ago or so, it was evident that Ibiza was attracting more and more super-wealthy people each summer season. The VIP trend was started in the early 2000s by various big-name celebrities coming to the island to get off their heads in style. This started a copycat trend for the younger element of the world's hedge fund managers, property developers, oligarchs' offspring and bankers who'd struck it rich to come and splurge vast sums of money on wildly hedonistic jaunts to the island.

So the local businesses put their prices up and up and up until one of the better-known beach bars was charging €1,200 a day for a normal beach-bed and far more for one in the VIP area – incidentally, imagine how mad it has to get in general for there to be a VIP area at a beach bar in the first place.

While this is not technically stealing, merely greedily ripping people off, it eventually makes it almost impossible to go out for the mass market customers; so the clubs get emptier and emptier, except on the really big nights, and eventually the whole island goes into decline and no one does well.

The summer season at the time of writing is showing all the signs of this now.

Furthermore, the way cause and effect seems to work is: you steal something from someone and someone else winds up stealing something from you, because it's all one big, intricately balanced continuum.

Eventually you grow so aware that your integrity is the most valuable resource you have, and so aware of the law of cause and effect, that you begin to see that stealing (even just fleecing people) only ends up weakening the very infrastructure you rely on for your survival and damaging yourself at the deepest level.

Eventually you evolve to such an extent you realise that you and everyone else are expressions of the Tao, God, in human form and that to steal is to steal from yourself.

But such awareness is not learned through force, and certainly not by any commandments being imposed on you. It only develops by becoming conscious in a global sense, and so developing respect for all parts of the continuum.

And this only truly occurs through gradually becoming more centered and hence awake.

This even applies to seasoned con artists, people suffering from kleptomania, 'professional' burglars and people stealing to fuel crack habits.

But as with desisting from violating or killing others, this process will take a long, long time. However, I learned it in my own life through the practice. If I can do it, so can everyone else.

Commandment/Precept/ Principle Nine

Thou shalt not bear false witness.

The greatest faculty we have is consciousness. Without it none of this would be here and we wouldn't be having this discussion.

To be able to bear witness to the show unfolding is the greatest gift we'll each ever know.

To distort this faculty by bearing witness falsely is to disown the gift, at least in that moment.

And the way cause and effect works, disown the gift and the gift disowns you back, leaving you utterly confused about what's what and what isn't.

Not that that's the end of the world in itself.

But adding to the convolution of lies presently governing our world is definitely not helpful to your own or the collective evolutionary thrust.

However, we're truly up against it with this one.

Ramakrishna, the great Indian teacher from two centuries back, suggested you didn't need yoga, meditation or any other form of practice to become enlightened. You just needed to be honest with everyone all the time – no exceptions. It's that simple. Too simple for most of us, however – hence the need for all the various spiritual practices.

Richard Bach, who wrote the modern-day bible *Illusions*, suggests, "To try to be true to anyone or anything else is not only impossible, but also the mark of a fake messiah."

That's because, whatever you say, there's necessarily another whole side you're not saying. Whatever you own up to, there's the other side you're holding. It's impossible to reveal the truth from every angle, because not only would you not have the time, but whatever you said would merely be subjective and not absolute.

Nonetheless, the web of lies perpetrated by politicians and the media today is absurd. The public expects it and would probably feel quite uncomfortable with any degree of the truth, anyway.

"We're on a train that's about to crash catastrophically and really haven't a clue what to do about it, so are obfuscating and pretending we do, just to mollify you and keep you distracted so you don't rise up in mob panic and create even more mayhem than we can presently cope with just now, meanwhile raising taxes just because we can." It simply wouldn't cut the mustard, statement-wise, in the daily news, however close to the mark it is.

So instead people talk loads and loads of endless shit.

And this runs through every stratum of society all the way round the world, except perhaps in Bhutan.

And it's always been so.

- God gave Moses the tablets.
- Jesus was conceived immaculately.
- Your country needs you! *(to die)*
- We drop bombs on Libya because we care about the people *(not the oil)*.
- I really do love and respect you and don't want this just to be a one-night stand *(him)*.
- I really don't want a relationship, I just want to have fun and I want you to be free *(her)*.
- Of course I don't fancy anyone else. I only want you *(him)*.
- Of course I don't fancy anyone else. I only want you *(her)*.
- There's no corruption and the police don't accept bribes.
- I must kill you in the name of God.
- Hold steady, this won't hurt a bit *(doctor about to inject you)*.

- I always look perfectly manicured, groomed and poised like this – and I don't ever do such disgusting things as void my bowels.
- Everything's OK with me, I'm doing fine.
- Of course I never masturbate or secretly look at porn.
- We have a perfect relationship, don't we darling, we're still very much in love after 30 years *(at the dinner party)*.
- God has a beard and will punish you if you don't obey his laws by sending you to eternal damnation in the fires of hell.
- If you blow yourself and loads of other people up, you'll have 72 virgins to keep you company on the other side.
- Of course I haven't had Botox *(my forehead's frozen like this naturally)*.
- Royal people and aristocrats have blue blood.
- The Jews killed Jesus *(not the Romans, who adopted Christianity and didn't want to look like the bad guys)*.
- I can make you thin.
- I can make you fat.

- We're enriching uranium for peaceful purposes *(Iran)*.

And on and on.

Lies, lies, lies.

The air's thick with them.

And has been for millennia.

So obviously this commandment has had as much effect as hanging a pair of underpants on a stick on the beach to stop a tidal wave.

However, the more you learn to center – the more you understand and accept that beneath the surface everyone is a manifestation of the same presence; that, subconsciously at least, everyone knows when you're lying, just as you know when they're lying; that lying to others merely denudes your own consciousness of authenticity; and that to add more lies to the mix only slows down and hinders the evolutionary thrust we depend on now for our collective survival – the less you will be inclined to lie.

As with all the ten principles of grace, you'll slip in and out of it along the way, but when you do, because you're evolving in self-love and acceptance, you will simply note the diminished sense of self that instantly ensues, acknowledge you don't enjoy it that much, and agree with yourself to be more vigilant about your options next time the temptation to lie arises. That way you will open the possibility that you'll choose the honest option more in future.

At root lies our innate fear of abandonment from the pack, the fear of earning the opprobrium of others and being sent into exile.

But as we evolve, we know more and more surely that, as an intrinsic node in the continuum, it's impossible to be abandoned. It's impossible to be sent into exile, as the presence of which you're the human expression is everywhere, forever and ever.

By and by, as more and more people gain enlightenment, the lies will slowly subside and eventually it's even possible we'll be able to tell each other the truth most of the time.

On the other hand, it really doesn't matter that much – it's all just theatre in the end. If the play is rife with dishonesty, obfuscation and hypocrisy, so be it – at least it's rivetingly entertaining.

But as more and more of us touch that place of absolute truth, deep at our core, we'll automatically project that onto life (which, after all, is merely a mirror reflecting back our inner landscapes). Truth will pervade far and wide, obliterating all but the tiniest residue of dishonesty (just for good measure and in honor of yin and yang), as far as the eye can see.

On the other hand, that could just be a lie.

Ask me in two hundred years.

Commandment/Precept/ Principle Ten

Thou shalt not covet your neighbor's wife, nor his male servant, nor his female servant, nor his ox, nor his donkey, nor anything that is your neighbor's.

Not even his yellow leopard skin hat.

Coveting (from the Latin *cupere*, to desire) in this instance means desiring something someone owns, or someone they're in any sort of relationship with, without regard for their rights or feelings in the matter.

Such coveting is in contravention of the first commandment: putting other gods before the all-embracing number one presence; being so consumed with desire for one particular form or expression of the presence that you forget the presence informing it, as well as the presence informing whoever has whatever it is you want, and so disregard feelings and propriety in your quest to obtain it for yourself. This in turn generally leads to contravention of the commandment not to steal, probably of the commandment not to lie, and possibly even of the commandment not to kill.

While not necessarily leading to crime, it constitutes a sin, in that you're obscuring your awareness of the presence within you and so preventing, obfuscating or losing your enlightenment, so blocking or decelerating the evolutionary thrust in yourself and, by extension, in everyone.

Not that the thrust isn't resilient or powerful enough to withstand it. But following the coveting urge does tend to lead to entrapment and opaqueness, as opposed to freedom and lightness of being, and causes pain and suffering to all concerned, including you.

But entrapment, opaqueness, pain and suffering are not the end of the world. If everything is operating according to any sort of preordained destiny, and all things work together to ultimately produce the highest good, they are exactly what the theatre of life decrees as necessary at that point. But it makes mess and mess slows you down, weighs you down and, in the extreme, brings you down.

But when you do get hooked on a desire for someone or something, a desire so anchored in your loins you can't override or sublimate it, it's obvious no commandment will sway you to desist in your desire, despite any guilt or shame it may elicit from you. You'll simply find a deft way of rationalising it and carry on regardless.

This isn't about being evil or bad; it's simply about being human – human with an ever-present option between choosing the path of action, which will gratify your desire yet slow you down, or the path of non-action, of containment of the desire, which will speed you on your journey of evolution.

The latter is not a path devoid of gratification. On the contrary, by letting go, centering and thereby flowing with the evolutionary thrust, all things and people requisite for your healthy growth and highest good will be manifest in your path. But these are not the source of your real fulfillment but merely the symbols of it. The real reward, the real fulfillment, can never be derived from anything or anyone external but only from your alignment, moment by moment, as you wend your way along the path, with the source of all of it: the Tao, the God, the OM, the Great Sympathy, the Great Blah, the presence.

Being able to let go of an inappropriate desire for something or someone invariably results in you receiving what's for you in a similar vein – your very own, original yellow leopard skin hat, for instance, instead of someone else's.

And this is always way better for you and your healthy growth than the object of the desire you've managed to override.

Let go of desiring your neighbor's donkey and you manifest a thoroughbred racehorse. Let go of wanting his ox and you manifest a top-of-the-range 4x4.

As for his male and female servants, or the modern equivalent – personal assistants, drivers, pilots, jet technicians, boat crews, housekeepers, chefs, cleaners, massage therapists, hypnotherapists, psychotherapists, Pilates instructors, personal fitness trainers, yoga instructors, life coaches, hairdressers, beauty technicians, nail technicians, pool attendants, and window cleaners – along with all the technological toys and equipment and other accoutrements of the billionaire lifestyle, just think of the wages you'd be paying out each month and give thanks you don't have that weight round your neck.

Naturally, let the lifestyles you admire be an inspiration, but resist the trap of envy, the driving force of any coveting tendencies.

Envy implies not believing in your own power or entitlement to manifest what you need for your own healthy growth and potential fulfillment, and so wanting to piggyback on someone else's ride and steal theirs.

Inspiration implies having evolved sufficiently to know your Tao, your path, your God, your OM, your Great Blah. More precisely, your relationship with it is a benign one that elicits a natural, spontaneous provision of all the resources you need to fulfill your potential as an expression of the Tao. Thus you will be able to contribute (and receive) the very most and best possible this lifetime.

This is the essence of *wu wei* – the ancient, time-tested Taoist method of manifesting whatever you need merely by setting the intention to do so and then allowing events to shape up themselves into the optimal configuration to produce the desired result. *Wu wei*, and how to use it to your best advantage, are explained extensively in my book *MANIFESTO*.

It rests on the premise espoused in that old Scottish axiom: "*What's for ye won't pass ye by, and what passes ye by wasn't for ye.*"

It implies being willing to trust the Tao to deliver whatever you need, whenever you need it.

And this implies knowing from your bones outwards that what you have right now, with all its inevitable lacks and flaws, is precisely what you need at this moment, even if you don't like it; and that beneath your preferential mind lies the miracle of your own existence, the constant appreciation of which constitutes the only genuine source of the quality of bliss your soul constantly yearns for. Hence it doesn't matter whether you get what you assume you want or not. It only matters that you appreciate the miracle of your existence as it's happening here and now.

This attenuates your grasping tendencies, which otherwise impede the *wu wei* delivery system.

But it also implies trusting that what others have is what they need, is exclusively a matter between them and their Tao and has absolutely nothing to do with you, except perhaps by way of inspiring you along a certain direction.

Hence there's no need or room for envy, no urge driving potential coveting tendencies. To the contrary, the urge becomes one of wishing everyone well, because that reaffirms your commitment to being able to manifest whatever you need for yourself.

However this state can only be attained from the centered state. Off-centered, you fall prey to envy and all the ills that ensue.

Of all the ten precepts for enlightenment, or principles of grace, this is perhaps the most poignant in respect of your interactions with humankind.

Imagine a world so evolved that whole nations are inspired by, rather than envious of, other nations. Imagine the advances that will be made, without recourse to diverting such hefty sums and material and intellectual resources as are presently diverted to the machinery of warfare.

It's possible – and even probable – if enough of us get the message of THE MESSAGE.

Section 3:
Vision for a New Golden Era

If a large asteroid collided with Earth and everything went up in one mighty puff of smoke – no more planet, no more us – what would happen to the things people believed sacrosanct, divinely ordained, divinely handed down: the Bibles, the different names for the Great Blah that cannot be named, the dogma, the myths, the litanies, the observances, the beliefs, the opinions, the stone tablets and all the rest of it?

What would still remain?

The universal principles underlying all the above.

What we're doing here is entertaining the notion of embodying them, as a stratagem for evolving to the next stage and being able to live together in a new world in a sustainable, healthy, joyful, loving, harmonious, prosperous way.

Grace arises naturally when you're in a centered state, achieved by daily training, and thus in command of yourself at the deepest level (the angelic level if you like).

Forgiveness arises naturally from grace.

Forgiveness means acknowledging that everyone is an expression of the presence; that each person or version is doing the very best he or she can according to his or her current state of evolution;

that if he or she could do better, he or she would; and, furthermore, that each is playing his or her role in the given theatre of life. None of these roles or their effects on your person are to be taken personally, no matter how convincingly to the contrary it often appears, but trans-personally: from the God or angelic presence within others to the God or angelic presence within you and vice versa.

Forgiveness doesn't mean forgetting or ceasing to hold to account. It simply means desisting from the urge to punish by way of seeking vengeance.

What would happen if forgiveness as a force became contagious to the point of a global forgiveness-pandemic so profound it thoroughly infected every stratum of global society, all the way to world-leader level?

What would happen if the desire for revenge for past wrongs was attenuated all the way down to an inaudible whimper?

Trust would emerge ubiquitously.

What would happen if trust in one another was ubiquitous?

We'd disarm.

What would happen if we disarmed in such a situation?

We'd channel the imponderable and unsustainable level of resources currently diverted into the machinery of warfare into generating a sustainably prosperous, harmonious, healthy, joyful, loving global society.

How would yin and yang come into play?

By lending the result a bit of grit and friction to stop it getting tedious and dull and so keep the story moving on for the entertainment of one and all.

And what we'd also find, as a result of a grace-fuelled forgiveness pandemic, would be an unprecedented shedding of lies and increase of honesty.

From honesty would come authenticity of communication, leading to a more fulfilling, joy-filled time of it for all, thus requiring fewer resources diverted to the business of diversion and liberating more resources to support our sustainable enterprise.

And from this globally joyful state would arise an attenuation of the need and relevance of externally imposed dogmas, commandments, morals and all the other manipulative, hypocrisy-engendering factors employed over the millennia by way of political control of populations.

And in the universal collective awareness of the one same presence informing us all, people would stop feeling the compulsion to use force, to dominate, to kill, to violate, to adulterate, to steal, to lie, to covet, and would instead be inclined to cooperate with one another, to produce what would probably be the most spectacular success ever known in this section of the universe.

When love is the currency, we no longer need religion or dogma; we no longer need crowd control of any kind.

From crisis comes both danger and opportunity.

The above is my version of the Aquarian vision – the gospel according to Barefoot; a vision of the Promised Land. I expect you have a version of your own or, if not, trust that you've been sufficiently inspired by what you've read to allow one to form itself.

I'm not going to say anything as crass as "together we can make it happen", firstly because such wildly bandied about clichés truly make me puke, and secondly because that's merely a cheap sentiment for fools.

We can't control errant earthbound asteroids, we can't control the natural forces, we can't even control our own financial systems; but, provided the dangers we're facing don't prove too overwhelming and we manage to survive them en masse, this book might well provide a viable template to expedite such a world.

And it's in that possibility that I'm placing my vote – not just for us and our children, but also for their children and their children's children, and on through the generations, even unto the end of the Age of Aquarius and beyond.

May it be so.

And thus spake Barefoot.

Appendix I
Definitions and Exercises

This chapter offers definitions and explanations of a few essential philosophical premises in order to clarify basic terms and references.

DEFINITIONS

The OM (AUM)

The OM (AUM) is one of my ways of referring to the subsonic aspect of the ineffable presence evidently, or presumably, informing this universe and goodness knows how many other universes, from the primordial, subatomic level, with the light of consciousness, energy and love. The *A* stands for the creation of all phenomena; the *U* for the sustaining of all phenomena; and the *M* for the inevitable eventual destruction of all phenomena, to make space for it all to start over again – and again and again ad infinitum. It's another way of saying Tao, God, Universe (with a capital *U* – though I confess to finding this particular name clumsy and in grave danger of becoming clichéd through a current trend towards careless overuse), Great Spirit, Prime Cause and any other name you care to ascribe to the ineffable.

The Tao

The Tao is the ancient Chinese word (pronounced with a soft *T* and *not* the coarser sound of a full *D)* for the ubiquitous, all-creating, all-informing, all-animating and all-connecting presence beyond words. It is variously translated as *The Way, The Great Way, The Great Flow, Mother of all existence and non-existence, the Great Sympathy, The Great Comedian* (translation peculiar to me) The Great Blah (likewise), *The Great Thoroughfare,* along with many other more obscure appellations. But however you translate it, you still come face to face with the advice in the first verse of all the myriad translations of the *Tao Te Ching*, the granddaddy of all Taoist literature, supposedly collated from the surviving remnants of Taoist oral tradition at the time by Lao Tsu, keeper of the official archives in Hunan Province nearly 3,000 years ago: *the Tao that can be named is not the true Tao.*

The Tao implies the sum total of all motion occurring throughout the universe at any one time (and at all times forever and ever), along with your perception of it, along with everyone else's perception of it, along with your reaction or response to your perception of it, along with everyone else's reaction or response to their perceptions of it, along with the motion of everything that isn't in this universe: the action on the other side of black holes, the alternative universes that may exist or not, along with the prime cause for all of it, and the whole thing collated as one universal entity.

Taoism

The pure form of Taoism I've practiced for over 40 years, and taught for the past 30 through all means possible, is in no way a religion. In fact to even ascribe an *ism* to it is anathema.

The beauty of pure Taoism is that its practice brings you directly into face-to-face contact with the Tao, the God, by engendering an instantaneous state of enlightenment. It requires no priest or intermediary, no organization or liturgy, no dogma, no faith, no belief, no mumbo jumbo, no silly vocal quirks, no bizarre, ritualised ticks or spasms and no obedience of any kind, other than to the immutable, inescapable universal laws of yin and yang.

It infers no original sin. To the contrary, its practice elicits a clear, direct awareness of being but a manifestation or expression of the one presence and so not separate or capable of sinning (literally missing the mark) in any way.

And while dialogue with the presence, the Tao, the God, is encouraged if it arises spontaneously (as opposed to by contrivance or forcing it) it *is* dialogue, meaning a two-way exchange, rather than a monologue-style supplication through prayer.

However, its practice at the master level mostly consists of training yourself on a daily basis in your chosen routine from a plethora of psychophysical techniques. This includes Tai Chi and the other, less well-known, Taoist martial arts Xing Yi and Pa Kua, along with qigong (chi gung), internal alchemy (meditation to gradually develop the *immortal spirit body*, the shape of the angelic presence within), positive-reframe techniques such as affirmations and visualizations, *wu wei* manifesting techniques, creativity-enhancement techniques (to encourage both a greater throughput of material from your muses and the skill to express the result with eloquence and elegance), self-applied stimulation of acupuncture points (by needling, acupressure, rubbing, stroking, kneading, percussing, pinching and chanting) and by *feng shui* techniques to create a stronger energetic alignment in your home and place of work.

And all of this is supported by an appreciation for the way in which the primordial forces of yin and yang command all aspects of manifest reality, and an ability to discern between the causative level and the manifest level at all times, as well as an ability to use the *chi*, the energy or kinetic force of the Tao in motion, thus being in the world but not of it.

Daily practice enables you to reference all experience to what's going on in your body as opposed to your thoughts. You can thus change the experience you're having by such levers as adjusting your breathing, your posture and the elasticity of your muscles, or positioning your awareness in different parts of your brain and so on.

Daily practice has a cumulative effect. In the fullness of time you learn to maintain a state of meditation at all times, while simultaneously engaged in the daily round: while walking, talking, implementing ideas, and fulfilling all your tasks and obligations. This affords you the ability to sustain an enlightened state at all times, whence derives the highly evasive bliss people normally seek in vain in externals. You can be in the world loving every minute, yet not of it, no longer deluded or entranced by the usual nonsense of seeking prestige, power, wealth, possessions, popularity and inclusion.

Along with this comes a natural amplification of your inner childlike, playful spirit. You become like a child again, but one who is able to self-conduct responsibly in the world. You play in life rather than struggle with life. As a result you enjoy it all a thousand times more.

Paradoxically, by letting go of the insane need to establish yourself as a permanent fixture and allowing your inner childlike playful spirit to take command, you become far more effective at the games of commerce and so on, and so elicit a far freer, more enjoyable lifestyle.

Mildly alarmingly – yet predictably in the light of the human tendency to make definitions then generate a set of rules and restrictions to guard those definitions, to make institutions out of a good idea, to create religions and thereby divisions – one stream of Taoism morphed into a quasi-religion about 400 years ago, complete with all the usual mumbo jumbo: Taoism for idiots. This is total anathema to the spirit of pure Taoism and the inherent danger of *isms*. Yet this aberration seems to be currently gaining ground: an intellectualization and conceptualization of Taoism as an avoidance of doing the actual practice. That's right: they're turning my Tao into a religion – they usually spell it prosaically as Daoism instead of elegantly with the far more lyrical *T* – and it troubles and embarrasses me in the same way it might have troubled and embarrassed Jesus to see his pure form of existentialism transformed into the muddle of what we now call Christianity.

Such is the way of the world, though I sincerely hope that some of those who might have been waylaid momentarily will be induced to explore the pure form through reading this very book.

God

An angry, old, gray-bearded bastard in the sky, who expects you to go all mealy-mouthed, say daft things, genuflect, suspend logical thought and believe in him as your father or lord, implying that you think of yourself as a worthless piece of shit. Maybe, then, he'll not drop an asteroid on your head; but if he does anyway, you have to thank him...?

Not at all. That's just the propaganda promulgated by those who wanted to take advantage of the gullible over the past six millennia or so: primitive magic, relying merely on superstition.

What about those who demand you kill or maim people who don't agree with the name you're calling him, to please him?

That's just the same old black magic presented in a different idiom.

And, alas, there are still many who remain deluded by all this, though I do believe this is just a phase, an aberration that will pass once we reach the next stage of evolution.

So what is God?

Same as the Tao, as far as I'm concerned.

No old man in the sky, no lord, no punishment or reward system for doing what you do or don't do, or for praying or not praying. No anthropomorphising whatsoever, as that really is in the realm of people acting like big babies. It's ridiculous – as ridiculous as the current tendency for spelling Taoism with a D and turning it into a religion.

I'd use the word *God* a lot more freely, as it was the name of the ineffable I grew up being used to, but the very word carries such a heavy, emotive, twisted load for most people that I generally desist. However words are just words, names just names: there really isn't any value in getting hung up on any of them, and they're certainly not worth fighting for.

We need to clarify here and now, that any ideas of any angry old bastards in the sky, leaning over the edges of clouds and passing down sets of stone tablets to other angry old bastards on mountaintops, after which the latter would have the strength to carry these heavy stone tablets back down their mountainsides, is patently absurd.

It's actually astonishing that any of this is worthy of pointing out, astonishing the world has been so entranced by absurdity for so long that it even has to be mentioned. But we do live in an absurdist-inclined world.

The Background Presence

This is the least loaded, most pragmatic, demystified, succinct, atheist-friendly way I know of describing or referring to the Tao, the God, the OM (AUM), the Great Blah. I've interchanged all these terms for the ineffable, and more, throughout, and place no special significance on any of them – they're just names for what cannot be defined. Names are just names, after all, none of them sacrosanct in themselves. For, as I said earlier, if an asteroid crashed into Earth and the whole lot vanished in a puff of smoke, where would those names be then? Would they still exist, hence do they indeed possess any inherent *a priori* essence of their own? I suggest not.

Religion

It appears the sequence is: someone gains enlightenment through practice, spontaneity or a combination of the two; they start teaching their method; their method gains agreement; it gets picked up by more and more people, who in turn each influence the original method, mostly by distorting it and watering it down; it continues to gain agreement with more and more people, gradually becoming something quite different to the original spirit of the thing; it goes through a process of formalization, structuring and institutionalising by its more fervent adherents; and it eventually morphs into its exact opposite – as, for instance, when the Crusaders wreaked havoc across the known world in the name of someone who espoused peace, forgiveness and turning the other cheek; when the Spanish Inquisition tortured systematically in the same name; or when the Jihadists randomly exploded self and others in the name of Allah.

Something starts out as a really good idea. Then, when enough people get involved and the collective level of consciousness descends to the lowest common denominator, it all gets messed up.

And the more blatant the mess, the more the purity of the original spark has been obscured, the more its adherents vehemently defend it to the point of indulging in complexes of lies so thick they're all but impenetrable.

This isn't to say that you can't follow the prescripts of any religion and be a peaceful, spiritually sound person, but you'd have been one anyway with or without the religion. I've met many people who have followed that path and then dropped the religion through disillusion to discover the (pure) Taoist-humanist approach instead. Once they started engaging in methods that granted direct access to the Tao (or God, or whatever you want to call it) without any intercession by intermediaries, their growth quantum leaped.

Nor is it to say that organised religions do no good on a social level, for there are countless instances of well-developed social support networks sponsored by the various religions.

However, the insistence by each religion, or at least most, that their way is the only way and all other ways are invalid or heretical, is, like racism, or the differential between rich and poor, one of the most, if not *the* most divisive and potentially destructive factors of human life, which is the exact opposite of what we need right now.

Of course, you can take the best from the philosophy and methods of whichever religion you inherit, adopt or are merely fascinated by and integrate it respectfully into your own template; but I suggest the blind swearing of allegiance to any particular creed or doctrine is generally regressive as far as both your individual growth and the evolution of the collective are concerned.

The Original Sin

The word *sin,* from ancient Greek, means the differential between the bull's eye on an archery target, and the place at which your arrow actually lands. The bull's eye represents the enlightened, awake, centered state, in which you're fully aware of the background presence, the Tao, the God, at all times and are so deeply in harmony with it and all its manifestations that nothing and no one can perturb, unsettle, confuse or in any way detract from your universal sense of wellbeing.

The arrow represents the trajectory between your intention and the resulting action.

And the distance between the two represents how far off the mark you are in that instance.

But it doesn't imply a crime – merely a falling short. It may well include a crime, but that's another matter. Sin in itself simply denotes missing the mark.

The original sin – eating of the tree of knowledge, the acquiring of self-consciousness and vanity – actually refers to the mistake (literally also meaning *missing the mark*) of assuming you're separate from the Tao, the Great Sympathy, hence somehow outside it and needing to get back to it through prayer or whatever other method. This is an illusion in the first place.

It's impossible to be apart from the continuum; impossible to be anything other than an expression of the same background presence that informs everyone else. Any drive to return to it is also illusory.

You could say enlightenment is remembering that you never really forgot in the first place.

But forgetting in the first place isn't a criminal act: it's just a delusion. It's not something to be punished for, or to punish yourself for; it's just something to snap out of in exactly the same way you snap out of a trance or a bad dream.

Angels

Given our well-honed propensity for devising the most nonsensical myths by which to live, it's no surprise that humongous measures of nonsense have been spouted over the years about angels, by unscrupulous people absurdly claiming actual knowledge of the angelic realm and preying on the weakness and gullibility of others.

However, despite all the fanciful conjecture, there are certain feelings we do seem to share in common about angels, so can assume some possibility for validity in: that they exist at all – this seems fairly universal; that there are a metaphorical hundred thousand on either side of you at any one time, all dancing on the head of a pin; that if you ask them for help sincerely and with good intention, they invariably oblige; that they move at the speed of light (hence the symbolism of the big white wings); and that they seem to coalesce into a multidimensional, pyramidal, hierarchical configuration or host.

No one can say if any of this, or anything else for that matter, constitutes absolute truth, and it doesn't matter in any case. If it feels right for you, as long as you don't foist your opinions about it on others to make money or gain kudos, it's as true as it needs to be to make things OK for you as you go along.

Whenever I've resorted to calling on the angels to help, the healings brought about on all levels and in all aspects of life, for myself and even more notably for others, are undeniable.

Now, whether angels are merely thought-forms collectively projected into the ether until they seem to take on a life of their own, or whether they exist as *a priori* entities, is immaterial as long as the model works for *you*.

And that's all well and good, but their relevance to this work is a different proposition altogether.

For what if we ourselves are the angels – angels who've taken human form and have 'fallen' to Earth – who only now are waking up to who we all really are?

What if evolution comprises acting from the angelic self, from the angelic presence within?

What if our mission, rather than being driven by an egocentric agenda, is instead driven by an urge to do what angels do: help, serve, heal and make good for whoever calls on them to do so?

What if our scapulae (shoulder blades) are indeed the origins of our invisible angel wings?

Let's assume they are.

Grace

The Taoists call the state of grace *teh* (pronounced *tay*), more normally translated as *virtue*. This is virtue in the original sense of being in a state of truthfulness with self and others and an implication of a foregrounding of the other nobler qualities too: valor, honor, kindness, courage, fairness and so on. It arises whenever you're centered and awake to the presence of the Tao within and around you, as well as within and around everyone and everything, aware of it at both the causative and manifest levels, and aware of it being but one universal entity expressing itself in a myriad of shapes.

It implies you're identified with the angelic presence within you, aspire to remain so for the duration and are thus aware and respectful of the angelic presence within everyone else too.

Inevitably you fall in and out of the state of *teh*, as you become distracted by the external movement of light, color and shape in the world of the ten thousand things. The art is to remain sufficiently mindful to pull yourself back into grace by using centering methods.

It's the state of *teh* or grace we're aspiring to elicit on a mass scale here through this exploration of its ten guiding principles.

The subconscious

What you're conscious of in any given moment is just the tip of the iceberg. The conscious mind's job is to précis what's occurring in the main body of mental activity occurring at the subconscious level and to rationalise it as best it can, to enable you to go about the business of staying alive and effective in the game. The subconscious is your own personal access point to the ubiquitous consciousness informing, linking and governing every aspect of the cosmos, from the minutest subatomic particle to the hugest galaxy.

Through your subconscious mind, you know everything that ever was, is and will be, without exception. You know what people are thinking, what they've thought and what they will think. You know the precise mechanics and mathematics of every single moving part comprising the manifest universe. You are privy to all the information there is.

The role of your conscious mind is to filter this down to the amount of information you can actually handle from moment to moment and to make some sort of sense out of it.

As will be explained when we come to the centering method, this gives rise to an ongoing internal dialogue consisting of a passing commentary and appraisal of what's being experienced and how it's shifting your position in the game. It's a constant gauging of how well or badly you're doing compared to others (normally to those you perceive as doing better than you) and compared to yourself (normally to those times you were doing really well); judgment of yourself, judgment of others; considerations of how you imagine you look in the eyes of others; considerations of what you'll wear for an upcoming event; how you'll do your hair; lists of the things you need or want to buy; wondering what you'll do today, tomorrow, three months hence; debating whether you're making the best of it or somehow missing out; wondering what you're missing out on; telling yourself you're stupid, telling yourself you're wonderful; fantasising various forms of escape; musing philosophically, examining your beliefs and opinions; and on and on and on.

And all of this, this whole opinion-based internal dialogue in the conscious mind occurs, spatially speaking, in the forebrain.

Over the past couple of thousand years or more, especially over the past few hundred and even more especially over the past fifty or so, this forebrain-based mental activity has gained such dominance that it's generally mistakenly accorded the commanding position in the mind even though it's entirely predicated on mere opinions and beliefs as opposed to actual knowing. We've grown accustomed to imagine we're guiding ourselves through life by it, when what actually guides us is the information being processed and the choices being made at the subconscious level.

Following the path of enlightenment could be explained as the process of opening up your conscious awareness to what's being processed and the direction being chosen at the subconscious level. The more you do so, the more you avail yourself of the stream of infallible intuition (literally tuition or guidance from within) arising from being privy to all the information in the universe.

One manifest example of this is playing the drums or percussion – any musical instrument, in fact, but the drums provide the most obvious instance. Playing complex rhythms requires counting beats and bars so quickly and efficiently that the conscious mind would never be able to accomplish it. It's all done at the subconscious level, where the mind is able to discern and utilise the underlying arithmetic of existence. The expert drummer merely *feels* the rhythm and is able to perform percussive feats way beyond the scope of the conscious mind.

Or take the example of an athlete about to do the high jump. The arithmetic, algebraic and geometric calculations required to make that jump are so complex that the conscious mind would never be able to achieve them in the run-up timeframe. The athlete merely *feels* her or his way into it.

In daily life, the more you allow this intuitive stream to be your guide, even and especially when it runs counter to what your rational mind's telling you, the more space you afford to the events of your life to spontaneously resolve themselves. This will produce a far more benign configuration (outcome or result) than when you're straining to push or pull life events into shape by force or contrivance.

You must be willing to remain empty so that you can respond to the internally arising prompts and remain in harmony with *The Great Flow*, rather than being so full of rationalising that you can only react emotionally to the externals and so force yourself along disharmonious lines. It implies adopting the acquiescent position at all times and following the flow of the river, rather than forging the river bed itself.

This describes the essence of the Taoist meta-stratagem for living a fulfilling, globally successful life.

It's how you allow the angelic presence within to take command.

What makes the Taoist method unique is the way it teaches you to reference the experience of being *you* to various regions within the actual body. The body (and not just the brain) is the arena in which your experience occurs and is processed.

Hence the subconscious, meaning literally *under the conscious mind*, is referenced to the upper brainstem region just under the midbrain, with an anchoring connection to the heart down below and, further down, to the lower abdominal area. The intuitive stream therefore originates deep in the belly, rises through the heart, passes through the upper brainstem region and emerges in the midbrain.

When we come to the explanation of the centering method, you'll find out exactly how to activate this flow and bring it to the light of conscious awareness.

When the intuitive stream becomes conscious, you're able to formulate your intentions for the sort of broad-based outcomes you desire: success, health, longevity, harmonious relationships (with yourself, with the people in your life, with your environment, with your financial flow and with all aspects of your external world), a joyful tone of mind, and so on. When you set your intention from the subconscious level, you invariably manifest the desired results, and you don't even have to know how; in fact you must desist from trying to figure it out at all. The Great Flow will take care of shunting all the relevant external factors into the optimal configuration to produce the result for you – all you have to do is follow along.

In this respect, the Taoists also suggest following along in the spirit of 'four ounces' (110 grams), implying that you think every thought and perform every action with utmost sensitivity and respect for all manifest parts of existence (because each is a holographic version of the whole, the Tao). You never push your will on people, events, or situations with more (or less) than the metaphorical four ounces, rather than the 'thousand pounds' more normally used when coming from the rational mind. Conversely, you never let people, events, or situations push you with more than four ounces. So you stick to the action using just four ounces and you yield to oncoming force, while holding your center, deftly enough that no exogenous pressure can impact on you with more (or less) than four ounces. It implies an ergonomic attitude free of self-importance and pride – a humble, yielding yet dignified, confident stance maintained at all times, as you wend your way along 'The Great Thoroughfare', your path through life.

It's this opening of the subconscious and the physiological changes it causes in the brain, that'll be the physical signpost and effect of the next stage of evolution.

Your path

The Tao, The Great Way, also refers to your own individual path, Tao or Dharma (as the Buddhists call it).

What determines your individual path is as mysterious as whatever it is that determines the path of existence in general. And while you can conjecture about intention, cause and effect, karma, benefits or disadvantages accrued from past lives, self-esteem and a sense of entitlement, no one ever has known, nor ever will know, the absolute truth. No one will ever know whether freedom as a primordial principle exists or is an illusion. No one knows whether you can change your fate or not, for while it certainly appears that you can, perhaps even the choices involved in doing so are destined, too.

And it really doesn't matter.

At best your experience of life can only be subjective.

But one thing is for sure, or at least has the appearance of being for sure: the Tao acts like a mirror onto which your beliefs are unconsciously or consciously projected and which, in turn, reflects those beliefs back at you as material manifestation points in linear time. In other words, life will always reflect your beliefs back at you; it will always confirm your beliefs by producing the exact results to reflect your beliefs about the way it has to be.

So if you believe you have a preordained path, life will reflect that back at you by getting events and situations to conspire to prove you right. And it doesn't matter if this is absolute truth or not. In this realm of appearances, the effect is the effect whether it's ultimately real or not.

And if you believe you have a guardian angel, spirit guide or even the Tao itself, pushing or pulling you along in any given direction, that's what life will reflect back at you and that's how it'll work.

This is the meaning of creating your own reality, or version of reality.

The way I experience it myself, after all these years of practice, is that my destiny is given. I seem to have a choice about the tone with which I wish to enjoy the experience – warm or cold, soft or hard, pleasurable or painful and so on. I seem to have a choice about optimising or minimising my experience and the value derived from moment to moment. The story, however, is somehow already written. My part, rather than making decisions or plans or attempting to forge a path, is to adopt the acquiescent stance and merely discern where the Tao or path is trying to lead me, with as little resistance as possible, flowing like water at all times, never piling up or going stagnant, capable of massing into a tidal wave yet able to remain as humble as a single raindrop.

The Tao and the world of the ten thousand things

At the causative level, there's the Tao. The Tao has been there causing existence (and non-existence) since before this universe came into being, and before the one before that, and the one before that, all the way back before even infinity came into being. It will continue to be here causing whatever is and isn't even after this universe has expired, and the one after that, and the one after that, and even beyond the point at which infinity ceases to be.

As far as the Tao's concerned it's on its own, even unto and beyond infinity and, empathising, you can imagine that gets repetitive and lonely. So it automatically generates existence along with its ever-proliferating myriad of discrete forms. It drops each living form an amnesia pill so it forgets it's the Tao, thus making it possible to play hide and seek, in order to keep itself entertained. For the Tao it's like playing with an imaginary friend and we have to understand we're nothing more than that. In essence we don't really exist. None of this really exists in an *a priori* sense. What we are is a collection of atoms that habituate themselves into a viable enough shape to create a form, albeit a passing form, for long enough to give us each a chance to wake up and remember we're actually the Tao throwing shapes in the mirror.

But the Tao is the consummate master of the game of hide and seek. No matter how deft we become at unmasking the Tao, it will always find more and more subtle and ingenious ways to distract us and make us forget again. This is why the physicists playing with the particle accelerator will never actually find the one so-called 'God particle'. Nonetheless, despite its playful compulsion, its deeper craving is for us all to eventually unmask it and remember that if we're anything at all, we are it. As soon as everyone remembers, the game will be up, the universe will all at once vanish and it'll start all over again.

So this universe, in all its unfathomable splendor and power, is nothing more or less than a gigantic magic lantern show, all its parts from the infinitesimally small to the imponderably large in constant motion, each subatomic particle a holographic version of the whole, giving rise to an infinite continuum of illusory appearances.

When you look at an orange, or a lemon for that matter, what you're actually observing is a process of decay caused by the underlying movement of subatomic and atomic particles. You, however, just see an object. This is a clue to why the Taoists call this the world of appearances or, more poetically, the world of the ten thousand things.

Nothing in it – nothing made manifest – is ultimately real. Everything is merely relative. The only thing that isn't relative and is ultimately real is the Tao, the prime cause of all of this.

And the point of knowing this, or adopting it as a model, is that by practicing meditation, by centering yourself, you develop a knowing that at your core you are that prime cause, you are the Tao, you are real. Once you know this, you're able to bear witness to the spin of external effects produced by the magic lantern show, without deluding yourself into believing you can gain any ultimate fulfillment or satisfaction from grasping onto any of them. You're able to draw your fulfillment and satisfaction from attuning to this causative level within and are thus no longer so perturbed by the inevitable rise and fall of fortune arising from the constant cycling of yin and yang (the alternating contractive and expansive tendencies governing the motion of all the infinite myriad of manifest parts of the universe). Instead you're able to enjoy them and even magic them into different configurations simply by seeing them so and willing it; but you're no longer fooled into believing that any specific configuration will elicit any more than passing fulfillment or satisfaction. How else could it be when all forms in the space-time medium are constantly changing?

The way the Tao generates this show is as follows.

The Tao is the one. The Tao becomes aware of itself. This awareness and the one make two. As soon as duality arises, yin and yang spring into being. Then the friction and fission generated by their constant cycling and alternation give rise to the 'five elements', metaphorically referred to as water, wood, fire, earth, and metal, describing the phases all phenomena cycle through – inception, growth, exegesis, stabilization and entropy.

These are the five so-called 'God particles' the physicists *have* discovered (respect to them). This is as far as the Tao will go in revealing itself.

And it's through the agency of these five elemental phases that the infinite numbers of myriad forms are given mass and shape and by which they're eventually dissolved.

And no matter how nimbly, adroitly and vigorously you rush around trying to organise external reality, you're onto a losing wicket, because everything is in motion. No sooner have you got one aspect to sit still for a moment and form a sensible shape to work with, than all the other parts spin out of alignment.

Hence the Taoist way to order reality is predicated on identifying with the center, the core, instead. Adjust the atmosphere and tone at the center and the external effects adjust themselves to match.

The outside invariably reflects the inside, in other words. It may take time, once you've adjusted yourself at the core, for the externals to move themselves into the corresponding configuration, but eventually everything in the world of the ten thousand things conforms to the balance of your inner space.

This means you can manifest your reality however you want it to be via intending it to be so, rather than attempting in vain to order it externally. Naturally, you have to do things out here in the world of the ten thousand things – you have to move about attending to your tasks and responsibilities, you have to communicate and so on – but in response to the inner urges arising from your core, as opposed to in reaction to the motion of external phenomena.

This not only grants you an easier, more peaceful, more fulfilling and more successful life, but it also plugs you in to the underlying glee of simply being here from moment to moment. Thus it initiates a state of perpetual bliss, which is precisely what everyone's looking for in vain all the while in the externals – the shopping, the amassing of wealth, the quest for good looks, prestige and status, the sex, the romance and all the other passing phantasms of the world of moving form.

As I said, I'll be explaining how to land at your center and hold it, thus taking full command of yourself, or allowing that angelic presence within to do so. You will have no further need for exogenously imposed commandments in due course, so don't just take all this as a mere theoretical proposition.

Empathy

On the way to the barn to write this book, I stopped for a refuel. I was buying something when a very stressed and distracted woman, pushing a baby in a pushchair, called out to me across the shop to ask if I knew which road to take to get to Swansea. We were on a parallel motorway, just a short right-angled hop from the motorway she wanted, at the end of which lay Swansea.

I could see she was in a mildly distressed state. She looked as if she hadn't had enough sleep for a while, as if she was panicking about money, as if she was fighting off a spike in the ongoing existential crisis and was losing, as if she was at the end of her tether. So I looked her in the eye, softened my heart to her, as if she was my daughter or some other beloved, watched her calm down a fraction, then explained the extraordinarily straightforward "turn next left, turn right straight after that and keep going" route with supreme clarity and simplicity, using visual clues to serve as mnemonic aids.

I could see it wasn't working and that she was just pretending to get the directions so as not to offend me, so I repeated them three times more, enough to elicit an almost Pavlovian response in most people. This time she acted comprehension well enough to semi-fool me.

I had to go to the ATM to withdraw some cash. As I got there, she was asking someone else, who was going through the motions, and she was still only pretending to understand. I discreetly did the ATM finger dance and pretended not to see her to save her embarrassment.

I could have gone into judgment, but I was empathising. This meant that while our interaction may have been fruitless directions-wise, it certainly afforded her a moment of feeling cared for and acknowledged.

What I see happening more and more is people managing less and less to hide their internal crisis, primarily from themselves and then from others.

The game is growing ever more stressful and people are traumatised by it, hence unable to receive the help they ask for. Meanwhile, as well as being a person with a story, she was symbolic, for instance, of how many people are asking for help – help to get more enlightened, to get out of debt, to get more effective, to manifest more, to get healthier – yet are panicking so much inside that they can't receive it when it's given. So they hop from pillar to post asking, thinking it will somehow accrue and take the place of actual help. It doesn't, and so the situation progressively worsens.

Nothing happens by accident, however. According to the belief system I subscribe to myself, everything is always working together for the highest good, no matter how contrary it may seem from time to time. So it's fair to surmise that the burgeoning individual and collective crisis occurring at every level is precisely what's required for the next stage of evolution to occur.

What you do is obviously entirely up to you, of course.

But because, through practice, I know I am merely an expression of the one presence, I also knew that the woman with the pushchair was an expression of it, and the baby in the pushchair too. So when I spoke to her, it was the angelic presence in me appealing to the angelic presence within her. And on the telepathic level – for telepathy is something that develops naturally and strongly as a byproduct of practice – I could hear, in my inner ear, her angelic presence assuring me that though she was geographically lost, our exchange had afforded her a moment of finding herself existentially. That moment would be enough to swing her around – enough to get her head working sufficiently to find her way home geographically as well.

The more centered you become through practice, the more naturally and easily you empathise with the others rather than judge them. When, in the fullness of time, everyone has developed this ability to at least a minimum extent, the ten principles or signs of grace will take a spontaneous hold of the collective, giving rise to an endogenously born set of ethics, as opposed to an exogenously imposed set of mores, based on the innate decency emanating from the angelic presence within, without any rules being enforced.

Appendix 2
The Seven Steps Of Grace

All Taoist martial arts, movement (*qigong/chi gung*) and meditation training begins with and is entirely informed by seven distinct steps, comprising a procedure you practice daily in a meditative way and subsequently reenact a thousand times throughout the day. The seven steps draw you back from the distractions of the world of the ten thousand things to your center again, and thus instigate and perpetuate a state of grace or *teh*, enabling the angelic presence within you to take and remain in command, as opposed to requiring any externally imposed commandments of any kind. They thus instigate a natural, spontaneous resonance with the angelic presence within everyone else, the key to future evolution, as well as your own personal fulfillment on the path – your fulfillment of your Tao or destiny.

The order the steps appear in is arbitrary, as they collectively comprise a cycle. This is the order I teach them in School for Warriors and it's proven itself, to me and my students over the years, to be as viable and efficacious as any, but feel free to juggle them at will once you know them. Be fluid and supple about whatever you do, including this.

Step one – let the angelic presence take command of your center

Gathering awareness of yourself in the lower abdominal area

When you want to thread a needle, you first have to lick and twist the end of the thread into a fine point so it can pass through the small hole. If the thread is you and this tiny hole represents your access point to the state of grace, whereby your angelic presence can take command of the show, gathering awareness of your lower abdominal area (specifically concentrated at a point just below and behind your navel) is the licked and twisted end of the thread.

Moving through life scattered, hence frayed at the tip, you'll never pass through the eye of the needle and will wander un-evolved, pulled hither and thither by the insubstantial, meaningless baubles and bangles of the world of the ten thousand things, through oceans of suffering till you die. Moreover, if scattered, you're never effective at doing what you do.

Observe any athlete, musician, leader of industry or expert in any field: when they're performing their tasks and meeting their challenges, they do so as a unified force – a single, focused entity. That way they achieve clear results. Scattered, you merely achieve scattered results.

The technique in this step is simply to think about your navel, or just a fraction below and behind it, and maintain at least half a thought on it all the time, no matter what else you're doing. I say simply, but in fact the art of remembering to do so is not easy. It requires willingness, patience, vigilance, attention and daily training.

But it's no big deal – just a simple matter of keeping half a thought on your navel region all the time. So whether you're talking, walking, sitting, getting up, lying down, turning over, washing, voiding your bowels, cooking food, making love, masturbating, meditating, martial arts-ing (especially then), typing, singing, playing an instrument or even just thinking, you do so from your navel: you think, talk, and act from your navel (or just a little below and behind it).

It doesn't seem much at first glance, but the internal, transformative effect is so profound over time, as your sense of center develops, that you eventually realise its greatness as a lever is as great as the greatness of the Tao itself.

This point just below and behind the navel is actually the physical center of your body. If you were a piece of luggage laid flat on your back, this would be the most ergonomic place to affix a handle and afford an easy lift.

If you were a wheel and this was your hub, it would make it a lot easier and less dizzying to situate your awareness here as you rolled along the road of life, than situating it anywhere on the periphery – the brain, for instance, which is where most people situate themselves most of the time, hence why everyone appears so fundamentally dizzy most of the time.

The Taoists call it your *tan t'ien*, meaning the field of heaven within you, implying that once fully activated, the heavenly or angelic presence is able to operate freely through you.

The *tan t'ien* provides the foundation, the seat of your subconscious mind, into which to anchor the entirety of your moment-to-moment experience of being you.

In summary, think about your *tan t'ien* and keep thinking about it all the time, with just half a thought, the whole day long as you work, rest and play and you'll be constantly optimising the whole enterprise of being you.

Step two - let the angelic presence take command of your breath

Nothing in life is more crucial than breathing. Once breathing stops, life as we know it stops with it.

Each out-breath expels the toxins from your system and releases the old and no longer useful.

Each in-breath introduces fresh life or *chi*.

Breathing is the most important thing in life.

That's basic and obvious. Everyone knows it.

What everyone doesn't know, however, is that it's also the most direct and immediate lever you have for changing your state of mind and physiology.

But first you have to stop holding your breath.

People unconsciously hold their breath in a vain attempt to hold the world still, presumably so nothing external can hurt or disturb them.

This is indicative of not appreciating that you're merely part of a continuum, in which there are no fundamental distinctions or divisions, in which you and others don't really exist as individuated entities, so ultimately there's nothing to hurt you and no one to hurt in the first place. But this heady notion need not be intellectually entertained or dissected at this stage – it will make itself clear through practice as time unfolds in any case.

Not only is it ineffective – you can't hold the world still, whether you and it are ultimately real or not – it also causes the exact opposite of the desired effect. For rather than the stillness and respite you crave, all it does is impede the circulation of blood and *chi* to the brain and other organs, thus constricting and stressing your system and your mind.

Holding the breath derives unconsciously from what Freud called the 'death urge'. It's a form of self-harming. When you're dead you're not breathing.

Stop holding your breath and let life flow freely, within and all around you. And train yourself to remember to keep your breath and life flowing freely all the time from now on.

The Taoists sages of yore reckoned each person was allotted a specific number of breaths, sufficient to last them a lifespan. If it's longevity you're after, slow your breathing down and stretch your lifespan.

But aside from this potential benefit, slowing down your breathing automatically slows down your mind, which in turn slows down your life, all of it to a sensible enough tempo to think and act in the most effective way.

When you panic or are riven with anxiety, as well as holding your breath, the breathing you *are* doing tends to accelerate to a pant.

Conversely, by slowing your breathing down you take the steam out of the panic or anxiety and your mind calms down so you can think clearly again.

Those old sages also reckoned that, because your lungs were so intimately related to the Tao or divine realm, breathing is also the key to remaining in the present moment, whence exclusively derives your personal power in any given situation. The out-breath relates to the past and its passing; the in-breath relates to the future you're moving into.

Evening out the length of the out-breath and in-breath thus places you firmly in the middle of the past and the future: the here and now.

The sages also prescribed adjusting the tone or quality of your breathing to adjust the tone and quality of your thoughts. Luxuriate in the sensuality of the breath passing in and out through your nose, as if reeling silk from a cocoon. Let it be fine, silent, subtle, silken and soft and your thoughts will more or less instantly become so too. And when the tone and quality of your thoughts become finer, more silent, more subtle, more silken and softer, the actual content of your thoughts, the things you're thinking about, become more positive naturally.

Finally, the more deeply you breathe, the more you deepen your experience of being you in any given moment and the more you're able to discern and appreciate the profound nature of existence from moment to moment, thus transforming your life as you go along.

But there are many misconceptions about what breathing deeply means and about the mechanics of breathing in general.

Correct breathing, meaning getting full use of the lungs, requires a totally opposite movement of the diaphragm (the transverse muscle in the upper abdominal area that works the lungs by making them bellow) to the one most people are used to.

Most people breathe into the chest alone, thus never moving the bottom parts of the lungs, the sumps where all the toxic detritus builds up.

The correct way entails the following.

1. Visualise a sponge filled with air in your lower abdomen.

2. Visualise squeezing the sponge by drawing the muscles of the belly backwards towards the spine, thus squeezing all the air out of it.

3. Now simply relax your belly and allow it to swell, like a pregnant woman's. The new air will come rushing in all by itself.

4. Gently contract your belly muscles and pull the belly back towards the spine to squeeze the sponge and expel the air. The in-breath happens by itself simply by relaxing the belly again.

Once you adopt this style of breathing, it will transform your entire experience of being you – it will change your life for the better forever.

To change the pattern takes about three weeks of practicing it, with your hands on your belly to guide the motion for nine breath cycles, once just after waking and once just before sleeping, after which you'll never look back.

Once you've got it going on down there, it links directly to the first step – thinking about your belly button – because that's precisely where the swelling-contracting motion is occurring, so you double the centering potential.

Step three - let the angelic presence take command of your posture

Optimising your mainframe

Adjusting your posture, by expanding your musculoskeletal structure, instantly adjusts and expands your sense of self, along with the power available to you in any single moment.

The four main bits of skeleton that require adjusting are:

- the spine – the one and only structure for supporting you in the upright position and for resting your head upon
- the shoulder girdle – the main breadth-giving structure and somewhere to hang your arms off
- the pelvic girdle (the hips) – the secondary breadth-giving structure and somewhere to attach your legs to
- the breastbone – there to protect your heart and lungs and stop your front caving in.

Through faulty postural habits, most people suffer some degree of both lordosis (forward curvature) and sclerosis (sideways skew) of the spine.

When, through lordosis, the head is inclined forwards, not balanced squarely on top of an aligned spine, your view of life inclines towards the ground. Metaphorically, this means you're looking down all the time which, as any mountaineer will tell you, is not the thing to do if you want to reach the peak. A downwardly inclined view of life promotes a pessimistic outlook.

When, through sclerosis, the head is titled to one side or the other, the view of life is also tilted and one-sided, encouraging a limited view of the possibilities available to you at any one time.

When the shoulder girdle is askew on account of hanging off a misaligned spinal column and constricted or narrowed by chronically raised shoulders (done unconsciously to protect the head from imaginary attack), the breathing and heart functions become constricted, thus depleting vitality and health and giving rise to emotional instability. Metaphorically speaking, you're less able to shoulder the burdens of life effectively. And by narrowing your body, you narrow your experience, narrow your thinking, and narrow your chances. Plus, when one shoulder is higher than the other, thus making the arm-reach uneven, you unbalance the flow between giving and taking (effected with the dominant and subdominant hand respectively).

When the pelvic girdle is constricted and askew from a combination of lordosis, sclerosis, pelvic floor tension (an unconscious misplaced survival mechanism for holding your shit together, figuratively and crudely speaking), you weaken your base and weaken the basis of everything you think, say and do.

When the breastbone is sunk, not only does it cause compression of the vital organs, thus depleting your health and vitality, it also makes you prone to feeling sunk and defeated.

None of this is to mention the deterioration of the actual bones and joints, or the excessive strains and chronic contractions, hence weakening of the various muscle groups involved, which have to work far harder to compensate for faulty skeletal structure.

By adjusting your posture with your mind, by lengthening the spine, you gradually correct the alignment, or at least stop the deterioration. By lengthening and realigning your spine so your head sits squarely atop, neither too far forwards nor too far back, not tilted to one side or the other, you're far more able to face life squarely with a balanced view of things, and more likely to see the goal rather than the possibility of defeat. In addition, the flow of blood and *chi* in and out of the head is improved dramatically, causing your brain to function more efficiently and your thinking to become clearer and more optimistic. And adopting the dignified (literally upright), commanding posture that comes naturally when the spine is lengthened, gives you more dignity and command over yourself and around other people.

By dropping and broadening the shoulder girdle, you're instantly more able and willing to shoulder your responsibilities, more able and willing to drop unnecessary burdens – beliefs, opinions, self-pity and grudges – and so lighten your spirit. You encourage a greater flow of blood and *chi* as well as allow more space for the heart and lungs to function more efficiently, which increases your health and vitality.

By broadening across the pelvic girdle, you broaden your base, you broaden the basis of your life and endeavors, and hence you broaden your options. Plus you encourage a healthier flow of blood and energy throughout your pelvic floor, which improves sexual and reproductive as well as eliminatory functions.

Finally, by slightly raising your breastbone, as if sliding it directly upwards a fraction rather than allowing it to cave in, you naturally raise your energetic vibration and find yourself resonating with the beauty within and all around you, rather than with the ugliness.

That's the model.

Now here's how to use it.

1. Having gathered yourself about your belly button and regulated your breathing, picture an invisible thread suspending the crown of your head to the ceiling or sky above, thus causing an elongation at the back of the neck and cervical region. Allow this elongation to affect the entire spinal column, subtly pulling all the way from the sacrum at the base of the spine, through the upper brainstem region and up through the crown of the head. Alternatively just push the back of your neck lightly back and slightly drop your chin. The main thing is to get the feeling your whole spine is suspended, lengthened and aligned.

2. Raise your shoulders up to your ears, then drop them. Do this as many times as necessary to get them all the way down. Then use your mind to broaden across the chest and shoulders. This happens by relaxing and softening the chest and letting go of the narrowness.

3. Relax your buttocks and pelvic floor and use your mind to broaden across the hips.

4. Finally, raise your breastbone – not much more than the width of a butterfly wing. Don't arch your back to do it, but just raise it enough to be subtly reaching upwards and slightly forwards.

You've now expanded your mainframe.

Like all the steps, it'll take a while to programme these changes of attitude and positioning into your deeper circuitry, but daily practice will take care of that for you.

Step four – let the angelic presence take command of your relaxation levels

Relaxation is one of the least understood activities there is – and it is an activity. Relaxing is a very different thing to collapsing. Relaxing means self-inducing a state wherein you're using the minimum level of energy and strength to achieve your goal, rather than using wasteful excess. This implies an innate trust in the Great Flow and that everything is constantly working to produce your highest good, so there's nothing to worry or stress over. Naturally this entails being willing to be courageous in the deepest sense, but conversely, by relaxing more, you naturally tend to elicit *teh*, whence springs courage along with all the other noble human qualities.

Relaxation means placing no undue strain on your body or mind by assuming the worst. It means assuming the best at all times and so not needing to armor yourself against potential pain by contracting the muscles unnecessarily.

Look at any pro athlete, extreme sportsperson (free-runners are a perfect example), martial artist, dancer or performer in action and you'll not see strain or stress – you'll see perfect relaxation in the midst of action. It would be impossible to perform their challenges effectively were they tense.

Naturally strength must be used, but only as much as is necessary and only in the muscle groups required to make whichever movement it is.

There's nothing floppy or collapsed about it. Perfect form is always aspired to, but there's no stress in attempting to achieve it – merely surrender.

This is *active* rather than *passive* relaxation, meaning you take it with you, or vice versa, as you do your work and engage in all the activities you engage in, as well as when at rest.

And rather than it entail anything arcane, esoteric or abstract in any way, it entails something entirely practical.

First, you develop a facility for scanning your body at high speed and detecting wherever you're gripping on for no actual reason. For instance, you may be gripping right now with your toes as you read this, and obviously you don't need strength in your toes to read a book, even one as demanding as this. Or you may be gripping at the back of the neck, which again is unnecessary when all you really have to move is your eyeballs, and even then only slightly.

Or you may be gripping with your jaw, when there's nothing at all to chew on except a few ideas, which the mind can process perfectly without any chewing action required.

In fact the main common areas of unnecessary gripping are the brow, ocular region, jaw, oral region, throat, back of the neck, shoulders, forearms, hands, fingers, thumbs, chest, upper belly, lower belly, between the shoulder blades, middle back, lower back, hips, pelvic floor, upper legs, calves, feet and toes.

And what you do is learn to scan swiftly from head to toe. The simple act of observing, coupled with an intention to let go, is enough to dispel a build-up of tension throughout the body.

Once you've told all offending muscle groups to let go and soften, do the same for your brain, nerves and sense organs, then your vital organs and bowels, then your blood vessels and other fluid-bearing channels, then your bones and finally even your bone marrow.

It does sound like a lot but with practice you very quickly learn to speed the process up so it can be done in the twinkling of a relaxed eye.

Then your mind instantly relaxes too, and all that dross you were churning round your forebrain, all those what-ifs, all those worries, all those fear-thoughts vanish into thin (inner) air, for they have no actual validity and won't hang on unless there's something tense to hook into. When you're fully soft, tension has nothing to hook into.

You can afford to do this without fear of falling over, because you've already attended to your structure and its optimal configuration in the previous step.

And from softness comes true strength. Softness, with its implications of suppleness, fluidity and flexibility, equates to life, hardness, with its implications of stiffness and rigidity equates to death. Choose life every time.

Keep breathing all the while, keep expanding the posture all the while, and keep thinking about your *tan t'ien*.

Step five – let the angelic presence take command of your connection to earth-plane reality

Sink to meet gravity

According to the Native Americans with whom I had the honor of living for four years as a younger man, the Earth is your mother and the sky your father.

The Earth is the mother ship: it supports you and gives you life, or at least a platform upon which to live your life; it feeds you, it entertains you and it carries you a few billion miles through space from the point of conception to the point of death. No one knows why it takes you on this journey through time and space; no one knows the purpose, other than to enjoy and make the most of every moment regardless. But as nothing happens by chance, as far as we know, there must be a damn good reason it picks your spirit up at one point in space and delivers it to another, and no doubt that'll make itself known when the moment's right.

Meanwhile, the Earth is hurtling along in orbit around the sun at no less than 35 kilometers (18.5 miles) a second, while spinning on its axis at 0.5 kilometers (0.3 miles) a second, as the sun and entire solar system hurtles along in orbit around the

Milky Way at 255 kilometers (155 miles) a second, and the entire galaxy goes at 300 kilometers (185 miles) a second.

Add that up and you get an imponderable speed; and you thought you were sitting, standing, lying, crouching fairly still, I bet.

All that kinetic power is available to you to channel through your body. It's moving through it anyway – you're just not aware of it. As soon as you become aware of it, you'll never be bored or restless or feel you're missing out again, for compared to that thrill, the lesser baubles and bangles of the world of the ten thousand things pale to insignificance.

And all you have to do to make it happen is to sink your weight and surrender to gravity.

Stop pulling away from the ground and instead trust your elongated spine to hold you upright. Allow all the weight in your head, shoulders and thoracic region to sink down through your hips, legs and feet if standing, through your sit-bones if sitting, or through your back if lying down, and allow it to sink all the way to the center of the Earth.

Not only will this give you access to the subtle yet imponderable power of the vast motion actually occurring, it will also help you make friends more with the material plane, thus improving your relationship with all its various aspects, including money and everything else that makes life sweet on the ground.

It will give you more gravitas, more rootedness, more patience and more harmony with your surroundings.

It will stop your thoughts racing, for once you start tuning into the actual speed occurring, you swiftly realise there's no point attempting to add to or match that with your own relatively puny speed of thought.

Paradoxically, attuning to the natural speed of the planet, solar system and galaxy slows you down.

And slowing down, rather than speeding up, is the only way to meet and greet the accelerating pace of life.

Step six – let the angelic presence take command of your consciousness:

Sliding the mind back into the midbrain

At the time of writing this sentence it's nearly midnight in the first week of July, yet this stone barn is positioned far enough north and west for the sky to still be bright – the sun hasn't set.

This next step has a similar effect internally – even when the thoughts turn to their darkest, there's always light, even though normally there wouldn't be.

It's perhaps the most exciting of all the steps and its effects are striking and profound. But it only works effectively, and is only safe to practice, once the preceding steps have been inculcated.

The risk otherwise is to inadvertently draw too much energy into the brain and cause psychic disturbance, mania or severe confusion.

You have to be grounded and fully relaxed to practice this with impunity and derive the desired result, which is nothing less than attaining and maintaining the fully transcendent state, beyond preference for pain or pleasure, inconvenience or convenience, failure or success, and even dying or staying alive.

I'll expand on this theme of being beyond preference as soon as I've done explaining the centering method, as it's fundamental to the full practice of letting go and following the Way.

Once you've achieved it you have nothing to lose, are free to play life fearlessly for all it's worth and are thus far more likely to win. Winning in the context of this book comprises you and every awakened person taking responsibility for everybody winning. The seventh and final step will help to direct you towards this.

Meanwhile, as you know, the constant internal dialogue by which you've hitherto attempted to ground yourself in reality occurs in the front of your brain. And no matter how disruptive to your peace of mind and emotional equilibrium, there's nothing you can do to stop it.

That's why it's pointless telling people who want to learn to meditate to still their minds.

This aspect of the mind will never be still.

But what you can do is draw your awareness backwards and out of the noise, by sliding it through the midbrain region till it's nestling up comfortably against the interior rear wall of your skull.

It's like entering a cave in the mountain peaks. Suddenly all the noise is so far away you can hardly hear a murmur.

Nestled up against the rear interior wall of the skull, you're able to gaze into the soothing void between and behind your eyes from way further back inside. Once you get used to it, with practice, you're able to do it with your eyes open too, so that while in the midst of activity, including all your dealings with others, no matter how stressful or delightful, you are able to remain in the meditative state all the while.

At first this internal backslide seems difficult to do, but only because you're used to treating the brain as something you think with, not something you feel from within or slide things about in. But once you get it, you realise it's the simplest thing in the world and that you actually knew how to do it all the time.

Visualisation is helpful in this. Imagine the inside of your skull is the interior of a cave high up in the sacred peaks. Sitting in it is a tiny Buddha with your face, perched on a pile of sumptuous, comfy, high-quality silk and satin cushions, leaning up comfortably against the rear wall of the cave, looking out through the mouth of the cave, situated just behind the bridge of your nose, along a line stretching into infinity through endless inner space.

As you visualise it, you start to feel it as a subtle physical sensation too, as if something's soothing and gently tickling you in the centre of the back part of your brain.

What you're actually doing is activating the energy in the pineal gland in the midbrain area – the third eye of Tibetan yoga, the terrace of the living for the Buddhists and the cave of the original spirit for the Taoists. But as it's such a subtle manoeuvre and such a short distance back from the forebrain, it makes it easier to overshoot all the way to the back of the head until it settles in the midbrain anyway.

It helps to gently push the rear of your neck back, too.

The best way to get it, as well as sitting with your eyes closed focusing on it (along with thinking about the belly button, breathing slowly and sensually, keeping the skeletal structure expanded, the muscles soft and the weight sunk, for the four minute daily practice session), is to do it frequently during the day as you work, rest and play, with your eyes open, perhaps 18 times an hour but just for a brief moment.

What you'll find is that you'll be pulled constantly forwards into the forebrain because you get distracted by the murmur of it passing its commentary and debating on the efficacy of what you're doing, or simply making a noise about something you need to do later or something someone said. The art is to stay awake to it and keep sliding it back inside the cave. Remember, however, that the visualisation of the little Buddha in the cave is merely that: a visualisation. What you're really looking for is that actual physical sensation gently tickling and soothing you from the middle to the rear of your brain. Once the sensation is established, it's relatively easy to keep doing it all the time. It just takes practice. (And it's worth it.)

However, aside from the danger of psychic disturbance, if not practicing it along with the preceding steps, there's the tendency to start feeling isolated and estranged from everyday society. Because once you attain the transcendent position, you are removing yourself from the usual level of concern for the relative trivia of the everyday. And that sets you apart from the majority, who at present still seem fully entranced by the everyday.

This is obviously counterproductive to the evolutionary experiment which requires that you now dedicate your practice and path to the coming together of all the peoples of the Earth as one, so that the Buddha can finally go home and get some well-earned rest.

And that's the significance of and reason for the seventh step.

Step seven – let the angelic presence take command of your capacity to give and receive love

Opening the heart

Opening the heart is the final key to the state of grace, to giving over to the angelic presence, both within you and within everyone.

For it is only in this interconnectedness that you or anyone else can flower, not to mention survive.

When your heart is closed to the world, your love stops flowing, the love of others can't reach you and you and your life shrivel, close down and die.

A closed heart comes about as a reaction to emotional trauma, usually as a child – trauma that wasn't processed effectively enough at the time and so lodged as tension in your chest and upper abdominal region, causing subtle yet actual contraction throughout the soft tissue surrounding and covering the breastbone, and connecting it to all the bits and pieces behind. This constriction subsequently increases progressively each time disappointment inevitably recurs, gradually causing the entire to calcify, to close over to form a fine, invisible but hard-to-penetrate sheet of armour.

If you practice the preceding six steps with a closed heart like this, the practice will exacerbate your sense of isolation and alienation and thus be counterproductive.

Conversely, if you practice this seventh step without the preceding steps, your love will be ungrounded, un-anchored to the truth of your being, hence dangerous in that you tend to end up giving the love inappropriately to those who would misuse it and drain yourself of life-force.

It's crucial to practice all seven steps in series, and preferably in the suggested sequence.

And when you get to the seventh in your practice, the rewards become obvious.

You're able to think from your heart, able to see yourself and the world through the eyes of love instead of fear, able to feel the connection to all that is in a milieu of warmth and safety. The confidence, fearlessness, courage and love you'll feel in your dealings with others will be astonishing.

So, having spared a thought for your navel, regulated your breathing, expanded your mainframe, softened your muscles and sinews, sunk your weight and slid your mind back to nestle up against the interior rear wall of your skull, visualise the two halves of your breastbone sliding open like a pair of sliding doors, to reveal your beautiful beating heart, whence is radiating a sea of rose-gold coloured vapour (love), with infinite streams of it passing both ways up and down the connection with the continuum of life – exchanging love with every sentient being, in other words.

Again, this is just a visualization and what you're really looking for is the actual physical sensation of disarming your chest area, removing the invisible layer of protection preventing you connecting with the world - a sensation of softening and deep relaxation throughout the thoracic region, from the center of the chest all the way up the thymus gland area at the top of the chest.

This is important as it reactivates the thymus, which otherwise tends to start atrophying at around the age of 21. The thymus is intimately connected to the excitement of the inner playful spirit, the child, the angelic presence, the pure self behind all the concocted layers of adulthood acquired over the years. It has a crucial role to play in strengthening the immune system and generating vitality.

Like thinking about the navel, however, feeling it initially requires great sensitivity and patience as it's such a subtle shift of focus; but as with the navel or sliding the mind back out of the forebrain, once you get it, you realise you always had it but just hadn't used it.

And as soon as you do open it and the love starts flowing freely up and down the connection, the transformation it wrings internally and consequently in all your interactions and relationships with others is as profound and radical as transformations get.

The dynamics become more flowing and harmonious; your innate desire to serve rather than grab comes naturally to the fore; the angelic presence takes over the show; healings abound; opportunities flow in abundance; others respond to you with love; the connections you make have more significance; your power to communicate increases exponentially; and those who would harm you shrink away from your light.

Of course this doesn't mean you stop being human, or that increased love-flow means you become a people pleaser. You'll still experience the full range of human emotions including anger, grief and sadness, but you'll no longer identify with them, invest in them or react to them.

This won't turn you into a saint or anything so one-dimensional, but it will imbue you with the undeniable sense that who and what you are is a nexus of life, love and consciousness in a continuum of life, love and consciousness (the Tao, the God, the OM, the background presence). It will set your dealings with others in a context of mutual empathy – compassion rather than mutual mistrust. This empathy will naturally give rise to a new endogenously arising set of ethics. The effects on your life, as well as on the world in general, will be startling.

The Final Word

God created the world in six days and on the seventh day He rested.

I wrote this book in six days.

And now I'm going to have a little lie-down myself.

Ta ta.

Barefoot Doctor, Angel Mountain, Pembrokeshire, West Wales, July 2011

Afterword

I am a time traveller.

And, as a time traveller – as well as getting to make a fortune on bets, high-five Jesus and prevent a war or two – I've been able to travel forwards six months to see what effect THE MESSAGE has had on you, dear reader.

And it's good news. I can't go into detail, as that would contravene the Time Travellers' Union code (in particular Item 4, Point c.). But that sense of freedom you're now feeling does persist. Barefoot's wise words stay with you. You do manage to practice the 7 steps every day. And the change in how you see the world creeps up on you slowly. But it can't be ignored. And it can't be reversed. After some weeks your heart opens, you can actually feel it doing so, and this means that – as well as seeing everyone and everything more compassionately – you begin to have an effect on other people. You feel more free and light. They begin to feel more free and light. Then they begin to influence others too. It's like a virus, but a good one.

Barefoot started it. You just got it. You now give it. And the world changes. That's how we enter a new golden era.

Honest, that's how it goes. I know. I've seen it already. And It Was Good.

John C. Parkin, time traveller and author of the Fk It books.**

Acknowledgements

Thanks to my mum for giving birth to me, to her and my dad for raising me, to all my ancestors for paving the way for that to happen, to the Tao for manifesting the whole thing in the first place, to everyone who has ever contributed anything to my life (including even the obstructers from whom I learned resilience), to my sons, Joe, Jake and Michael for being such huge shining lights, to Claire and Ed London for the wonderful Miami interlude, to all my friends, especially Jeb and Mike for the Welsh mountain fastness, Spencer Mac for always taking care of me beyond the call of duty and for helping create the book cover, Raja Ram for his ever-loving mentorship, brilliance and encouragement, John Parkin for so lovingly and magnificently sharing his Italian hillside and creative genius, and for his magnificent afterword, Rachel Elnaugh for being the bees knees top dollar manager, Jude Levy and Kat Dever at Imago for backing this, Ed Peppitt for all his invaluable and expert publishing work, Sue Okell for her utter loving staunchness throughout, Alan Davidson for being a giddy yet fabulous sturdy rock and for sorting out the Houston assignation so wonderfully, Juliette Chalmers for her angelically given Oxford fastness and invaluable edit work, Sally Stevens for her edit work, Craig for the French mountain fastness, Lucy for her glorious shining light and opening the gates of the Cote d'Azur, all the wonderful women of Monaco – Bolton, Candice, Jolly Holly, Sami and all for their wonderful kindness and friendship, Jeff Hessing for his shining wit, opening the joys of Nice up and doing the Jeff 'n' Steph music project with me, Jay Palmer for his shining example of going for it, his love and the Ibiza palace episodes, Marinela Ciftelli for keeping Ibiza warm, Tina Cutler for her everlasting love and being a truly magnificent woman, Andy Simons for keeping it musical with the Hofer66 feats Barefoot project, Ohm-g for keeping it cinematic, Jinny for making it safe, Stacey for the Mill Hill pit stop head reshuffles, Claire Light for the shire light, Heulwan Haf for the Cardiff fastness and her unshakable grace and support, Juliette Owen for her constant sparkle and word-spreading, SOS for the helping me sort the Barefoot Essence, Michael Lenz for helping with the original book, Daisy for the pit-stop reframes, and to all my School for Warriors students past and present for their invaluable feedback and willingness to participate, to all the Barefoot Satsang attendees past and present for sharing in the world-healing experiment, to all the wonderful people who follow me for making all this be possible, to all the friends and helpers I've inadvertently omitted to mention and last but not least, to me for being so cooperative and such an utter joy to work with throughout.

Also by Barefoot Doctor

Books

Handbook for the Urban Warrior

Handbook for Heroes

Handbook for Modern Lovers

Return of the Urban Warrior

Liberation

108 Blessings

Twisted Fables for Twisted Minds

Manifesto

Invincibility Training

Dear Barefoot

Tao of Sexual Massage

100 Lessons In Personal Attraction

Pure

The Man Who Drove With His Eyes Closed

Supercharged Taoist

Online Meditation

Weekly Online Satsang – www.barefootsatsang.com

Online Courses

School for Warriors Part I – principles of personal power

School for Warriors Part II – developing, harnessing and focusing chi

School for Warriors Part III – advanced consciousness training

www.schoolforwarriors.com

Workshops

Taoist Energy Medicine

The Tao of Sound and Movement

Tai Chi primer

Sound Healing

Wu Wei Manifesting

Music

Sound Healing (Medicinal Music)

Green Rabbit – Dance Meditation

Hofer66 featuring Barefoot Doctor

Barefoot & Leakster

Barefoot Presents Jeff 'n' Steph – Electric Window – coming soon

Barefoot Doctor – The Big OM – coming soon

Club and Party Events

Get Healed While You Party

Positive Message Sound Healing

Barefoot Doctor's Geisha Palace

Barefoot Doctor's Travelling Medicine Show

The Big OM

CD and DVD trainings

The Way of the Urban Warrior – Nightingale Conant

Learn to Meditate - Nightingale Conant

Jewels of Enlightenment - Nightingale Conant

For details on all the above visit www.barefootdoctorglobal.com where you can also sign up to join his global tribe of followers.

Imago People TV

Imago People is the TV based marketing portal created in 2011 by Rachel Elnaugh, Jude Levy and Katharine Dever, providing a platform to promote and market the products and services of transformational teachers, evolutionaries and heart-centred thought leaders.

The imago cells are the cells within a caterpillar, which hold the image of the butterfly. When the time for transformation arrives, the imago cells vibrate at a higher frequency and join together to trigger the process of metamorphosis.

Our ultimate vision is to create a global brand with the power to transform the lives of millions and raise the consciousness of the planet.

We also offer a full management service for established Imagoans and are proud to have signed Barefoot Doctor as our first 'star'. 'The Message' is our first published book and a DVD of Barefoot's UK debut performance of 'The Message' at Sadler's Wells will be available from March 2012.

If you are established in the transformation sector and would be interested in being part of Imago People TV please contact us at imagine@imagopeople.tv

If you are starting out on your journey and would like our help in getting your personal brand established, you may wish to consider joining the Imago Mentoring Cocoon – all the details are at www.imagopeople.tv/cocoon

To keep up to date with all the developments at Imago People TV please register at www.imagopeople.tv

We look forward to hearing from you.

With love,

Rachel, Jude & Kat